OXFORD
UNIVERSITY PRESS

INSPIRE
EXCEED
PROGRESS

Essential
Accounting
for Cambridge IGCSE® & O Level
Workbook
Third Edition

David Austen
Christine Gilchrist
Peter Hailstone

Oxford excellence for Cambridge IGCSE® & O Level

OXFORD
UNIVERSITY PRESS

Great Clarendon Street, Oxford, OX2 6DP, United Kingdom

Oxford University Press is a department of the University of Oxford. It furthers the University's objective of excellence in research, scholarship, and education by publishing worldwide. Oxford is a registered trade mark of Oxford University Press in the UK and in certain other countries

British Library Cataloguing in Publication Data
Data available

978-019-842831-2

10 9 8 7 6 5 4 3 2 1

Paper used in the production of this book is a natural, recyclableproduct made from wood grown in sustainable forests. The manufacturing process conforms to the environmental regulations of the country of origin.

Printed in Great Britain by CPI Group (UK) Ltd., Croydon CR0 4YY

Acknowledgements
Cover image: isak55/Shutterstock.

Although we have made every effort to trace and contact all copyright holders before publication this has not been possible in all cases. If notified, the publisher will rectify any errors or omissions at the earliest opportunity.
Links to third party websites are provided by Oxford in good faith and for information only. Oxford disclaims any responsibility for the materials contained in any third party website referenced in this work.

Contents

Introduction

Welcome to this *Cambridge IGCSE® and O Level Essential Accounting Workbook*.
It is a well-known fact that success in accounting goes hand-in-hand with plenty of appropriate practice. In almost every case the student who achieves their potential will have devoted much time to answering questions of differing types which cover all aspects of the specification. This workbook has been designed to offer students additional opportunities to develop their knowledge and understanding of accounting principles and their skills in applying accounting techniques.

The workbook has the following key features:

- **Comprehensive coverage** of the Cambridge IGCSE and O Level Accounting specification.

- A **variety of question types** including multiple choice questions, shorter-answer and longer-answer questions that require both computational and prose responses. The longer-answer questions start with a clear description of the knowledge and techniques being tested to help you select the questions most relevant to your learning needs.

- **Close links** to the textbook *Essential Accounting for Cambridge IGCSE and O Level* (3rd edition), so that you can refer back to the textbook for support when necessary.

- **Questions range from the simple to the complex** – there are questions which are relatively straightforward to help you develop your confidence, and questions which are more complex to provide a challenge for you.

- **Guidance notes** have been provided for the longer-answer questions – these notes provide support when necessary to help you get started on a topic which is perhaps less familiar or on a topic which has not been studied for some time. Guidance notes also cover the more difficult aspects of the question or common pitfalls.

- **Improving your performance** – Section 13 includes some advice to help you make good progress in this subject and to help you achieve your learning goals.

- **Answers to every question** – every question has been answered in full by the authors, so that you can check your own work immediately.

Introduction

In this first section you will have an opportunity to test yourself on the purposes of accounting, the basics of the double-entry system and the preparation of trial balances. It should be noted that the section covers these areas of knowledge in the simplest form only. Section 2, which follows, will test your understanding of the double-entry system in a deeper and more comprehensive manner.

Special note

When you answer the longer-answer questions in this (and all other) sections, try to avoid using the guidance if you are feeling reasonably confident. However, if you are feeling uncertain or think you may need some support, do have a look at this information shown at the end of the question. The guidance notes are there to:

- help you get started
- alert you to some of the more demanding aspects of the question
- remind you of how to avoid some of the errors that can be made when answering the question.

Multiple Choice Questions

1 Which of the following accounting tasks is the most unlikely to be undertaken by a bookkeeper?

  a Extract key financial details from invoices and other source documents

  b Keep day-to-day records of a business's financial transactions

  c Prepare a trial balance to test the accuracy of the double-entry records

  d Present financial statements for the use of the owner of the business

2 The owner of a business has just counted the day's cash takings.
What double entry should be made in the ledger accounts for this transaction?

	Debit	Credit
a	Bank	Sales
b	Cash	Sales
c	Sales	Bank
d	Sales	Cash

3 The owner of a general store recently purchased some office equipment and paid by cheque.
What double-entry record should be made of this transaction?

	Debit	Credit
a	Bank	Office equipment
b	Bank	Purchases
c	Office equipment	Bank
d	Purchases	Bank

4 A trial balance is being prepared. Which of the following is the correct list of account balances to be entered on the credit side of the trial balance?

  a Bank overdraft, capital, sales, trade payables

  b Bank overdraft, capital, sales, trade receivables

  c Drawings, capital, sales, trade receivables

  d Insurance, capital, sales, trade payables

Shorter-Answer Questions

5 Describe **three** main reasons for maintaining accounting records.

6 Complete the table below by stating which account should be debited and which account credited for each of the transactions listed.

	Transaction	Debit	Credit
a	Transferred business's cash to bank account		
b	Owner withdrew cash for personal use		
c	Sold goods on credit		
d	Received cash from a credit customer		
e	Sold some unwanted office equipment for cash		
f	A bank loan was arranged and the funds were transferred to the business's bank account		
g	Purchased goods for resale on credit		

7 State the main reason for preparing a trial balance.

8 The following table contains a list of some of the accounts to be shown in a business's trial balance. Complete the table by indicating in which column the balance of each of the accounts should be shown. Write 'debit' or 'credit' in the space provided.

	Account title	Debit/Credit
a	Capital	
b	Cash at bank	
c	Drawings	
d	Interest on loan from bank	
e	Loan from bank	
f	Purchases	
g	Sales	
h	Trade payables	
i	Trade receivables	
j	Wages	

Longer-Answer Questions

9 *Preparing basic ledger accounts from a list of transactions*

Morad owns a retail business. He sells bicycles and cycling accessories. The following balances appeared in the business's books at 1 May 2018:

	$
Cash at bank	4 580
Loan from bank	8 000
Shop equipment and furniture	18 460

a Calculate the business's capital at 1 May 2018.

b Open accounts to record the balances at 1 May 2018.

The following transactions occurred during May:

May	2	Purchased goods for resale on credit, $17 400
	6	Goods were sold for $8300 on credit
	7	Morad withdrew a cheque for $750 for private use
	8	Additional office furniture was purchased for $1840; payment was made by cheque
	11	Rent was paid by cheque $840
	13	Trade payables were paid $14 300 by cheque in part settlement of the amount due
	17	Goods were sold for $2930 and a cheque for this amount was received
	20	Morad repaid $1000 of the bank loan; funds were transferred from the business's bank account
	23	A cheque for $5800 was received from credit customers in part settlement of the amount due
	25	Some unwanted office equipment was sold for $250 and a cheque for this amount was received

c Record these transactions in ledger accounts.

GUIDANCE

This question provides a chance to record some straightforward transactions. When you get started remember that asset accounts have debit balances, whereas liability and capital accounts have credit balances. You can use the 'accounting equation' to calculate the missing capital figure. Do not forget that every transaction requires two entries to be made in the accounts. A debit entry should be made to record increases in assets, decreases in liabilities and capital (such as drawings, expenses, purchases). A credit entry should be made to record decreases in assets, increase in liabilities and capital (such as sales). Take care to record a date and correct narrative (name the other account) for each transaction.

10 *Identifying transactions recorded in ledger accounts*

The following accounts show a record of eleven transactions in the books of a retailer on consecutive days in August 2018.

Dr			Bank account				Cr
Aug	3	Bank loan	11 000	Aug	1	Purchases	3 700
	6	Cash	1 700		8	Trade payables	4 800
	9	Trade receivables	4 140		10	Cash	500
					11	Loan interest	100

Dr			Cash account				Cr
Aug	5	Sales	1 900	Aug	6	Bank	1 700
	10	Bank	500		7	Drawings	150

Dr			Drawings account		Cr
Aug	7	Cash	150		

Dr		Loan account				Cr
			Aug	3	Bank	11 000

Dr			Loan interest account		Cr
Aug	11	Bank	100		

Dr			Purchases account		Cr
Aug	1	Bank	3 700		
	4	Trade payables	6 200		

Dr		Sales account				Cr
			Aug	2	Trade receivables	4 140
				5	Cash	1 900

Dr			Trade payables				Cr
Aug	8	Bank	4 800	Aug	4	Purchases	6 200

Dr			Trade receivables				Cr
Aug	2	Sales	4 140	Aug	9	Bank	4 140

Identify the transactions which occurred on each of the days from 1 August to 11 August 2018.

> ### GUIDANCE
>
> It is important to explain fully each transaction to make it clear exactly what has happened. It would not be enough for Aug 7, for example, to just say 'drawings': you need to identify whether the drawings were in cash or from the bank account. In the case of sales and purchases, make it clear whether they were on credit or whether they involved cash or cheques.

11 *Preparing a trial balance*

Jasmine has extracted the following balances from her business's ledger accounts on 31 December 2018.

	$
Administration expenses	6 780
Bank overdraft	1 910
Capital	56 000
Cash in hand	130
Drawings	13 540
Loan from bank	10 000
Non-current assets	75 400
Purchases	62 390
Sales	110 480
Trade payables	5 470
Trade receivables	7 380
Wages and salaries	18 240

Prepare a trial balance dated 31 December 2018.

GUIDANCE

Do not forget to present the trial balance well by giving a full title and labelling the money columns Dr and Cr etc. Remember that assets, expenses and drawings have debit balances; capital, liabilities and sales have credit balances.

---

12 *Preparing basic ledger accounts and extracting a trial balance*

The following trial balance was extracted from the books of account of the business owned by Bobby Campbell on 31 July 2018.

	Dr	Cr
	$	$
Bank	3 740	
Bank loan		6 000
Capital		44 380
Cash	390	
Drawings	18 330	
General expenses	2 200	
Loan interest	480	
Motor vehicles	32 400	
Purchases	39 010	
Rent	5 570	
Sales		59 880
Trade payables		3 390
Trade receivables	2 680	
Wages	8 850	
	113 650	113 650

a Draw up the ledger accounts and record the opening balances at 1 August 2018.

The following transactions occurred during August 2018.

Aug	2	Bobby withdrew cash $230 for private use
	3	Purchases of goods for resale were made on credit $3850
	4	Received a cheque from a trade receivable $1070
	6	An amount of $80 was deducted from the bank account for loan interest
	9	Cash sales totalled $1720
	10	Transferred cash $600 to the business's bank account
	12	Sales on credit totalled $6340
	14	Paid trade payables $2800 by cheque
	18	Bobby paid $3500 into the business bank account from his private funds
	22	Repaid $1400 of bank loan by transfer from the business's bank account
	24	Paid general expenses in cash $330
	27	Purchased an additional motor vehicle and paid by cheque $7200
	28	Paid rent by cheque $610
	30	Paid wages in cash $840

b Record these transactions in the ledger accounts.

c Prepare a trial balance dated 31 August 2018.

GUIDANCE

When working through the transactions remember to pay careful attention to whether the transaction is on credit, affects the cash account or affects the bank account. It is a common mistake to record a cash transaction in the bank account, for example. Take care when calculating the closing balance on each of the ledger accounts when preparing the trial balance: the smallest error will mean that your trial balance totals will not agree.

Introduction

In this section you will have a chance to test yourself on the fully developed double-entry bookkeeping system. There are questions to test your skills in preparing bookkeeping records including:

- business documents
- books of prime entry
- ledger accounts.

Financial information is first received on business documents. The financial information is then recorded on a regular basis in the seven books of prime entry. Most of these entries are made on a daily basis.

The financial information is then posted to accounts in the ledgers, using the double-entry system of bookkeeping. There are three ledgers: Sales, Purchases and Nominal.

The double entry system of bookkeeping requires that every transaction is recorded twice in the appropriate ledger: once on the debit side of one account and once on the credit side of another account.

Multiple Choice Questions

1 What is a purpose of a credit note?

  a Record assets bought on credit

  b Record damaged goods returned to a supplier

  c Record goods bought on credit

  d Record goods sold on credit

2 What is the purpose of the purchases journal?

  a Record all goods bought for resale

  b Record goods bought on credit for resale

  c Record goods returned by a customer

  d Record goods sold on credit

3 The totals of the analysis columns in a petty cash book were:

	$
Stationery	15.40
Postage	10.20
Travel	12.30
Purchases ledger	25.00

The imprest is $100. What amount is required to reimburse the imprest?

  a $37.10

  b $37.90

  c $62.90

  d £100.00

4 The owner has taken goods for his own private use. What entry is required in the general journal?

   a Dr – drawings   Cr – bank

   b Dr – drawings   Cr – inventory

   c Dr – drawings   Cr – purchases

   d Dr – drawings   Cr – sales

5 A business buys a motor vehicle on credit from P Green. What double entry should be made to record this?

   a Dr – motor vehicles   Cr – P Green

   b Dr – motor vehicles   Cr – purchases

   c Dr – P Green   Cr – capital

   d Dr – purchases   Cr – motor vehicles

6 Goods bought on credit were returned to B Cope. What double entry should be made to record this?

   a Dr – B Cope   Cr – purchases

   b Dr – B Cope   Cr – purchases returns

   c Dr – purchases   Cr – B Cope

   d Dr – purchases returns   Cr – B Cope

7 Eric buys goods on credit costing $800, less trade discount of 25% and cash discount of 2.5%. What amount will he pay if he makes the payment within the settlement period?

   a $585   **b** $600   **c** $615   **d** $780

8 Goods were sold on credit $240, less 33⅓% trade discount. The customer returned some faulty goods costing $84. What should the final total on the credit note be?

   a $52   **b** $56   **c** $84   **d** $156

Shorter-Answer Questions

9 Sam owns a sports shop. During June he received the following purchase invoices and credit notes.

Date		Supplier	Invoice number	Cost $	Trade discount %
Jun	4	Blacks Ltd	731	1 320	20
	8	T Harvey	207	2 400	33⅓%
	15	M Brown	P113	940	15
	26	J Williams	314X	560	10
	29	T Harvey	222	1 500	33⅓%

Date		Supplier	Credit Note number	Cost $
Jun	20	T Harvey	52	270 gross
	30	J Williams	10C	80 gross

   a For the month of June prepare the:

      i purchases journal

      ii purchases returns journal.

   b Post the entries to the personal accounts in the purchases ledger.

   c Post the entries to the nominal accounts in the nominal ledger.

10 The sales journal and sales returns journal for Jack for the month of July are given below:

Sales Journal			
Date	Customer	Invoice number	$
Jul 3	P Watson	716	734
8	L Johnson	717	2 370
12	A Hunter	718	1 432
20	P Watson	719	845
24	A Hunter	720	433
28	L Johnson	721	940
	Total sales		6 754

Sales Returns Journal			
Date	Customer	Credit note number	$
Jul 7	P Watson	114	135
18	L Johnson	115	250
22	A Hunter	116	74
	Total sales returns		459

Post the entries to:

a the personal accounts in the sales ledger

b the nominal accounts in the nominal ledger.

Longer-Answer Questions

11 *Preparing a petty cash book*

Gill keeps a petty cash book. On 1 March the imprest was $200. The analysis columns are: postage, stationery, office expenses and purchases ledger accounts.

During March the following transactions took place.

Date	Transaction	Voucher number	$
Mar 3	Stationery	121	7.90
5	G Down	122	24.60
7	Postage	123	11.50
10	Office cleaning	124	15.00
12	Stationery	125	32.30
16	L Bennett	126	29.70
20	Postage	127	5.20
24	Office expenses	128	8.40
28	L Price	129	13.00
30	Postage	130	1.40

a Prepare the petty cash book for March.

b Balance the petty cash book at 31 March, and restore the imprest by cheque.

(See page 10 for Guidance)

12 *Preparing entries in the general journal*

Prepare journal entries, with suitable narratives, to record the following transactions in the general journal.

Aug	1	The owner of a business opened his books of account with the following assets and liabilities: fixtures and fittings $18 000, motor vehicle $5000, inventory $7200, trade payables $6300, bank overdraft $2400
	3	Purchased a motor vehicle on credit from L Walker $2500, invoice number 69
	8	The owner of a business took goods for personal use $125
	15	Sales on credit to J Peters $390 had been entered in T Porter's account
	20	Sold equipment $250 on credit to P Webb, invoice number 1235
	31	Purchases for the month $25 000 transferred to the income statement
	31	Discount received for the month $170 transferred to the income statement

13 *Identifying books of prime entry*

S Grundy maintains all seven books of prime (original) entry. The following transactions took place during September.

a Paid a trade payable by cheque

b Received an invoice for goods bought on credit

c Received an invoice for equipment bought on credit, for use in the business

d Paid wages by cheque

e Issued a credit note to a customer

f Corrected an error where a sale on credit had been entered in the wrong person's account

g Issued a voucher for a small amount of cash paid for postage

h Issued an invoice to a customer for goods sold on credit

i Transferred cash into the bank

j Received a credit note from a supplier

Name the book of prime (original) entry in which **each** transaction should be recorded.

> *GUIDANCE*
>
> *Take care to name each book correctly. So do not write 'petty cash' which is not precise, write 'petty cash book'; do not write 'purchases book', write 'purchases journal', etc.*

14 *Identifying source documents*

A business's policy is that any payment above $20 should be paid by cheque. Any amount below this is paid through the petty cash book.

The following transactions took place during the first week in February.

a Purchases on credit $150

b Cash sales $320

c Sales on credit $540

d Bank charges for the month $180

e Paid wages $230

f Cheque received from a customer $118

g Payment for postage $15

h Returned goods to a supplier $64

i Customer returned goods $104

j New office furniture bought on credit $3 000

Name the source document for **each** transaction.

> *GUIDANCE*
>
> *Give a precise answer. For example 'cheque' is not quite right. The precise answer is 'cheque counterfoil'. 'Invoice' is vague. Instead write 'purchases invoice' or 'sales invoice' as the case may be.*

15 *Preparing the sales and sales returns journal, calculating trade discount, and posting entries to the ledger*

Alice has a wholesale business. The following credit sales and returns took place during the month of January.

Jan 3 P Platt $360, less 20% trade discount, invoice no 231

9 A Lodge $1 200, less 33⅓% trade discount, invoice no 232

11 L Fox, $2 600, less 40% trade discount, invoice no 233

15 P Platt $120, (goods sold on Jan 3), credit note no 94

18 P Platt $870, less 20% trade discount, invoice 234

20 L Fox $200 (goods sold on Jan 11), credit note no 95

25 J Jackson $490, less 10% trade discount, invoice 235

a Prepare the following for January:

 i sales journal

 ii sales returns journal.

b Post entries to the personal accounts in the sales ledger.

c Post entries to the nominal accounts in the nominal ledger.

d State **one** reason why L Fox would be given higher trade discount than other customers.

(See page 12 for Guidance)

> **GUIDANCE**
>
> *When calculating 33⅓% discount, divide the amount by 3. Do not key into your calculator 33.3, as this will give a slightly incorrect answer. Do not forget to deduct the original trade discount from the sales returns.*

16 *Preparing a two-column cash book and naming source documents*

Bill Rogers keeps a two-column cash book. On 1 March the balance of cash in hand was $105 and the cash at bank was $460.

The following transactions took place during March.

Mar   3   Cash sales $1140

       7   Paid wages in cash £220

       8   Paid Tom Lee $740 by cheque

       9   Paid M Lewis $75 by cheque

     10   Cash sales $1850

     11   Paid cash into bank $1500

     15   Received a cheque from L Reid $2100

     19   Paid general expenses by cheque $84

     20   Paid postage by cash $24

     24   Received a cheque from Paul Smith $290

     25   Bought fixtures and fittings, paid by cheque $2830

     26   Bill Rogers took cash for private use $150

     28   Bank charges for month $56

a Prepare the cash book for March. Balance the book and carry down the balances at 1 April.

b Name the type of entry which took place on 11 March.

c Name the source document for each entry.

d Explain why there can never be a credit balance on the cash account.

> **GUIDANCE**
>
> *It is important to make sure that each entry has a date and a correct narrative. It is easy to miss out information, so do back over your work when you have finished: are all the entries dated? Do all the entries have a narrative? Remember to carry down the closing balances and remember that balances should be clearly labelled as c/d or b/d as appropriate.*

17 *Preparing a three-column cash book, calculating cash discount, posting entries to the ledger*

The following balances were in the books of Chana at 1 August 2018.

	$
Cash at bank	1650
Cash in hand	125
Trade payables:	
P White	1200
Jack Black	880
Trade receivables:	
A Chang	250
Sally Wong	3100

During August the following transactions took place:

Aug 2   Paid Jack Black by cheque, less 5% cash discount

     4   Paid general expenses in cash $34

     6   Received a cheque from A Chang, less 2% cash discount

     7   Cash sales $850

     11   Paid wages in cash $180

     13   Cash sales $460

     14   Paid cash in to the bank $600

     15   Chana took cash for private use $100

     18   Paid P White by cheque, less 4% cash discount

     20   Bought equipment by cheque $1000

     22   Received a cheque from Sally Wong, less 2% cash discount

     24   Cash purchases $56

     28   Paid insurance in cash $160

     30   Repaid loan by cheque $1500

a   Prepare the three-column cash book for June.

b   Post the details of the personal accounts to the sales ledger and the purchases ledger.

c   Post the totals of the discount columns to the nominal ledger.

> *GUIDANCE*
>
> *Remember to carry down the closing balances on the cash and bank accounts.*
> *The discount columns are not accounts, so they are not balanced. They are totalled separately.*

18 *Preparing a three-column cash book*

Pat Morris keeps a three-column cash book. On 1 April, the balances were: cash in hand $236 and cash at bank £420 overdrawn.

The transactions for April were:

Apr 1   Cash sales $380

     2   Received a cheque from R Mills in full settlement of amount owed $550, less 2% cash discount.

     4   Cash purchases $220

     6   Paid insurance by cheque $194

     10   Paid a cheque to B Bell in full settlement of amount owed $350, less 4% cash discount

     12   Interest received from investment $60 paid into the bank

     13   Paid wages in cash $150

     15   Received a cheque from B Price in full settlement of amount owed $400, less 2% cash discount

     16   Cash sales $810

     20   Paid a cheque to V Slater in full settlement of amount owed $850, less 2% cash discount

     24   Paid electricity by cheque $108

     25   Cash sales $750

     26   Bought equipment $1000 paid by cheque

     28   Paid cash into the bank $1400

a Prepare the three-column cash book for the month of April.

b Explain **two** differences between cash discount and trade discount.

> **GUIDANCE**
>
> *Each entry requires a date and a narrative. Note that the opening bank balance is overdrawn, and should be placed on the credit side. Check carefully before balancing the bank account, as the closing balance may also be overdrawn. Remember to carry down the closing cash and bank balances. The discount columns are not accounts, so they are totalled separately. When answering* **b** *make sure to name the discount being described. Also ensure that you explain a* **difference** *between the two types of discount, by referring to some key feature of each type of discount.*

19 *Preparing a supplier's ledger account*

Mary buys goods on a monthly basis from her supplier T Hall. On 1 May 2018 she owed him $680.

During May the following transactions took place.

May	4	Bought goods on credit $420, less 33⅓% trade discount
	10	Returned some goods $96 bought on credit on 4 May
	15	Paid a cheque to T Hall in full settlement of the amount owed on 1 May, less 2.5% cash discount
	24	Purchased goods on credit $330, less 33⅓% trade discount.

Prepare T Hall's account as it would appear in Mary's purchases ledger.

> **GUIDANCE**
>
> *Do not forget to balance the account at the end of the month, and bring the closing balance down.*

20 *Preparing a customer's ledger account*

Richard Park is a customer of W Ltd. The balance on his account on 1 April 2018 was $750.

The following transactions took place during April.

Apr	3	Sold goods $580, less 20% trade discount
	8	Received a cheque less 2% cash discount in full settlement of the amount owed on 1 April
	15	Sold goods $960, less 30% trade discount
	25	Richard Park returned goods $120, sold on 3 April

Prepare Richard Park's account as it would appear in Wilson's sales ledger.

> **GUIDANCE**
>
> *When balancing the account, ensure each balance is correctly labelled by including b/d and c/d as appropriate.*

21 *Preparing entries in the general journal*

a Prepare journal entries, with narratives, for the following transactions:

i B Shaw commenced trading with: equipment $6000, motor vehicles $9500, inventory $11 900, cash in hand $100, trade payables $2000, bank loan $3000 and bank overdraft $1800.

ii A cheque for wages was entered in the cash book as $157 instead of $275.

iii Sold old equipment to P Wood on credit, at its book value of $4000. On the same day bought new equipment $8000 on credit from LP Stores.

iv A customer, Bill Jones, who owed $640 had been declared bankrupt and his account had to be written off.

v A cheque received from John Gibson $300 had been entered on the credit side of the bank account.

vi Depreciation of 15% per annum had to be charged on fixtures and fittings, using the straight line method. The closing balance on the fixtures and fittings account was $3400.

b Explain when the general journal will be used to record transactions.

> **GUIDANCE**
>
> *Do not forget that each journal entry must be dated, and consist of a debit entry, a credit entry and a narrative.*

22 *Preparing all the books of prime entry, posting to the ledger, and extracting a trial balance*

Alex Jones opened a business on 1 January 2018. His assets and liabilities on that date were:

	$
Cash at bank	480
Cash in hand	150
Equipment	6 000
Motor vehicle	12 000
Bank loan	8 000

During January the following transactions took place.

Jan	3	Purchased goods on credit from P Moore full price $1800, less 25% trade discount
	6	Cash purchases $230
	7	Returned goods to P Moore full price $200
	8	Cash sales $650
	10	Credit sales to A Hill full price $1400, less 20% trade discount
	11	Cash sales $425
	12	Paid wages in cash $85
	14	Paid general expenses by cheque $45
	15	Paid cash into the bank $800
	17	Credit purchases from B Wright $840, less 20% trade discount
	20	Credit sales to C Parker $900, less 20% trade discount
	24	A Hill returned goods full price $160
	25	Alex Jones took cash $60 for private use
	26	Paid a cheque to P Moore for amount owing $1200, less 2% cash discount
	27	Repaid bank loan by cheque $400
	28	Paid rent by cheque $180
	29	Bought equipment on credit from J Carter $500, invoice no P74
	30	Alex Jones took goods $200 for private use
	30	Received a cheque from C Parker for the amount owing for goods bought on 20 January, less 2.5% cash discount
	31	Interest on the bank loan $54

a Prepare an opening journal entry to calculate the capital.

b Prepare the following books of prime (original) entry for January 2018:

i General journal

ii Three-column cash book

iii Purchases journal

iv Purchases returns journal

v Sales journal

vi Sales returns journal

c Post the entries from the books of prime entry to the appropriate ledgers.

d Prepare a trial balance at 31 January 2018.

> *GUIDANCE*
>
> *This is a large-scale question to test all the skills relevant to double-entry bookkeeping. To help ensure accuracy, be systematic. So work through the transactions in the order given, recording each in the appropriate book of prime entry first. Do not forget to total the purchases, sales and returns journals and the discount columns in the cash book at the end of the month. When you have recorded all the transactions in the books of prime entry, move on to posting to ledger accounts. It is easy to forget to post the totals of the purchases, sales, returns journals and the totals of the discounts columns.*

23 *Preparing entries in the general journal*

Prepare journal entries for the following transactions. Narratives are **not** required.

a The owner of a business opened his books of account with the following: equipment $10 000, fixtures and fittings $6500, motor vehicle $8000, inventory $4500, cash in hand $250, trade payables $3000 and cash at bank $1500 (Cr)

b Purchased equipment on credit from Andrew Sharp $2300

c Sold some fixtures and fittings on credit to Shan Ltd $800

d A credit sale of $340 to Susan Grey had been incorrectly recorded in Brenda Grey's account

e Returned some faulty equipment bought on credit $250 from Andrew Sharp

f A cheque paid for insurance $250 was recorded on the debit side of the bank account

g A customer Soo Ling who owed $540 had been declared bankrupt. The balance on her account had to be written off.

h Depreciation of 20% per annum had to be charged on motor vehicles, using the reducing balance method of depreciation. The balance on the motor vehicles account was $15 000, and the balance on the provision for depreciation of motor vehicles was $4000.

j The total revenue for the year $36 700 was transferred to the income statement.

k The balance of $650 on the advertising account was transferred to the income statement.

> *GUIDANCE*
>
> *Remember to ensure that the debit entry precedes the credit entry. Note that narratives are not required in your answer.*

Introduction

In this section there are questions to test your understanding of errors that will affect the balancing of the trial balance and those that will not. You will also test your knowledge of preparing journal entries to correct errors and how these are processed through the suspense account. Finally, you will prepare statements to correct draft profits and draft statements of financial position.

Multiple Choice Questions

1 Zara entered the payment for property rent into the property repairs account in error. What type of error is this?

a Error of commission

b Error of omission

c Error of original entry

d Error of principle

2 Sharon entered the payment for a new motor vehicle into the motor repairs account in error. What type of error is this?

a Error of commission

b Error of omission

c Error of original entry

d Error of principle

3 A cheque payment of $65 to a trade payable was recorded in the cash book as $56. What type of error is this?

a Error of commission

b Error of complete reversal

c Error of omission

d Error of original entry

4 Sammy has prepared his income statement for the year showing a profit for the year of $33 600. He has now discovered the following two errors.

i An accrual for wages of $1400 has been omitted

ii A prepayment for rent has been understated by $500.

What is the correct profit for the year?

a $31 700

b $32 700

c $34 500

d $35 500

5 Assam has prepared his income statement for the year showing a profit for the year of $58 100. He has now discovered the following two errors.

i The depreciation charge for the year has been understated by $3000.

ii Carriage inwards of $800 was incorrectly added to the gross profit.

What is the correct profit for the year?

a $53 500

b $54 300

c $55 900

d $56 700

Shorter-Answer Questions

6 Explain briefly the difference between:

a an error of commission and an error of principle

b an error of omission and an error of original entry.

7 Explain why an error of original entry does not affect the balancing of the trial balance.

8 Explain briefly the purpose of a suspense account.

9 A cheque received for $200 from Ayre Ltd was debited to Ayre Ltd sales ledger account and credited to bank account. Make the journal entry to correct this error.

Longer-Answer Questions

10 *Correcting errors not revealed by the trial balance*

The following errors were made by an accounts clerk in the current financial year.

i A cheque payment of $480 for a motor repair was posted to the debit of rent and rates account.

ii A cheque payment of $1260 for insurance was completely overlooked.

iii A cheque receipt of $415 from T Rogers was credited to the account of T Rogerson.

iv A cheque payment of £1450 for plant and machinery had been posted to the debit of repairs and maintenance.

v A purchase invoice for $230 for stationery from Paper Supplies Ltd, a credit supplier, had been entered in the records as $320.

a Identify the type of error in each of the above cases.

b Prepare journal entries to correct each of the above errors.

> GUIDANCE
>
> *None of the above errors affect the agreement of the trial balance totals, so a suspense account is not required. You may find it a good idea to quickly draft the accounts concerned and record the errors described. This may help you visualise the corrections that are required. Don't forget that a narrative is required for each journal entry (unless the question specifically states otherwise) and that it is a good idea to name the type of error concerned as part of each narrative.*

11 *Correcting errors revealed by the trial balance*

An accounts clerk was unable to get the totals of the trial balance to agree. The totals were Dr $38 850, Cr $39 050. A suspense account has been opened and debited with the difference. The following errors have now been discovered:

i The sales journal was overcast by $200.

ii Interest received of $130 has been correctly entered in the cash book but has not been posted to the interest received account.

iii A cash payment of $25 for postage has been correctly entered in the cash book but has not been posted to the postage account.

iv A sales invoice for $105 to G Boyd, a credit customer had been correctly entered in the sales journal, but had not been posted to G Boyd's account in the sales ledger.

a Prepare journal entries to correct these errors.

b Prepare the suspense account.

> *GUIDANCE*
>
> *All of these errors do affect the agreement of the trial balance totals. When you have prepared the journal entries to correct the errors, open the suspense account with the difference on the trial balance and enter the relevant parts of the journal into the suspense account. The suspense account should then balance as there are no errors left to correct and the totals of a redrafted trial balance would agree.*

12 *Correcting errors involving the suspense account where the difference in the trial balance totals is unknown*

The totals of a business's trial balance did not agree. Subsequently, the following errors were discovered.

i A cheque payment of $440 for repairs was entered correctly in the cash book, but not posted to repairs.

ii The sales returns journal was undercast by $100.

iii A cheque received of $290 from Zac Charles, a credit customer, had been entered correctly in the cash book, but had not been posted to Zac Charles' account.

a Prepare journal entries to correct these errors.

b Prepare the suspense account and identify the original difference in the trial balance totals.

> *GUIDANCE*
>
> *All of the above errors affect the balancing of the trial balance. After preparing the journal entries, post the necessary entries to a suspense account and the balance on this account will be the original difference in the trial balance totals.*

13 *Correcting errors, some of which affect the suspense account*

An accounts clerk was unable to get the totals of the trial balance to agree. The totals were Dr $46 020 Cr $46 240. The following errors have now been discovered.

i A sales invoice for $360 for Evans had been incorrectly posted to the sales ledger account of Evison.

ii The total of the discounts received column in the cash book had been undercast by $200.

iii A receipt of $120 for interest received had been posted to the debit of interest received account and the credit of bank account.

iv A cheque payment of $180 for motor repairs had been correctly entered in the cash book but had been posted to the motor repairs account as $160.

a Prepare journal entries to correct the errors.

b Prepare the suspense account.

> *GUIDANCE*
>
> *This question contains a mixture of errors, some requiring an entry in a suspense account and some not affecting the agreement of the trial balance totals. Start by deciding into which category each error falls before preparing journal entries. Any error not requiring an entry in the suspense account will be one of the six named types of error (commission, omission, compensating, principle, original entry, reversal).*

14 *Correcting errors, some of which affect the suspense account*

An accounts clerk was unable to get the totals of the trial balance to agree. The totals were Dr $60 750 Cr $60 960. The following errors have now been discovered:

i A cheque payment for heat and light of $220 had been debited in the cash book and credited to the heat and light account.

ii The total of the purchases returns day book had been overcast by $300.

iii Sales returns of $380 had been credited to the account of David Bishop instead of David Barton.

iv Cash sales of $450 had not been recorded in the accounting records.

v A cheque payment of $120 for stationery had been correctly entered in the cash book, but had been entered in the stationery account as $210.

a Prepare journal entries to correct the errors.

b Prepare the suspense account.

> *GUIDANCE*
>
> *Once again, not all of these errors will affect the balancing of the trial balance. Pay particular attention to the first of the errors – the debit and credit entries are the wrong way round. It is a common error for the wrong amount to be recorded for this type of error.*

15 *Correcting a draft profit figure*

Sara has prepared her income statement for the year ended 31 August 2018. The income statement showed a net profit of $38 300. The following errors have now been discovered.

i Rent of $2500 had been prepaid but no adjustment had been made.

ii Revenue had been overstated by $1900.

iii Depreciation of $4800 had been completely omitted from the income statement.

iv Advertising costs owing of $300 were overlooked when preparing the income statement.

Prepare a statement showing the effect of correcting these errors on the profit for the year.

> *GUIDANCE*
>
> *Start your statement with the original profit for the year of $38 300 and consider whether each error will increase or reduce that figure. The final result should be labelled 'revised profit for the year'.*

16 *Correcting a draft loss figure*

Erik has prepared his income statement for the year ended 31 July 2018. The income statement shows a loss of $2700.

i Discount received of $700 had been incorrectly deducted from the gross profit.

ii The accrual for heat and light had been overstated by $500.

iii Cash sales of $13 600 had been completely omitted from the accounting records.

iv An accrual for bank interest paid of $800 had been overlooked.

v The prepayment for rent had been understated by $4500.

Prepare a statement showing the effect of correcting these errors on the loss for the year.

> *GUIDANCE*
>
> *Remember, this statement will commence with a loss, not a profit. It is a common error not to make it clear how each correction affects the opening draft profit/loss.*

17 *Correcting a draft statement of financial position.*

Harry has prepared the following statement of financial position for his business at 31 May 2018.

	$	$
Non-current assets at net book value		55 000
Current assets		
Inventory	10 000	
Trade receivables	13 000	
Other receivables	3 000	
Cash at bank	8 000	34 000
Suspense account		1 000
Total assets		90 000
Capital		
Opening balance	42 000	
Add profit for the year	46 000	
	88 000	
Less drawings	28 000	60 000
Current liabilities		
Trade payables	26 000	
Other payables	4 000	30 000
		90 000

Harry has discovered that the following errors have been made while preparing the financial statements.

i A prepayment of $2000 on property rental has been adjusted in the income statement but has not been accounted for in the statement of financial position.

ii Closing inventory has been overvalued by $5000 in both the income statement and the statement of financial position.

iii An accrual for wages of $1000 has been adjusted in the income statement but has not been accounted for in the statement of financial position.

iv An irrecoverable debt of $3000 to be written off has not been accounted for in either the income statement or the statement of financial position.

Prepare a correct statement of financial position at 31 May 2018.

GUIDANCE

Remember, if an error has not been accounted for in both the income statement and the statement of financial position, it will not affect the suspense account, but it will affect the profit for the year. It is a common error not to provide detailed workings to show how the new figure for profit for the year was achieved.

Introduction

In this section there are questions to test your understanding of two processes which help verify accounting records:

- bank reconciliation: you will have the opportunity to answer questions which require you to update cash books and prepare bank reconciliation statements and write about the purpose and use of these processes.
- control accounts: questions are included on the preparation of purchases ledger and sales ledger control accounts (including making entries for some more unusual transactions) and on the purpose of this process.

Multiple Choice Questions

1 Raju was preparing his business's bank reconciliation statement and he was aware of the following details.

- Uncredited deposits $1900.
- Bank balance in the cash book $6700 debit.
- Unpresented cheques $2300.

What is the balance shown on the bank statement?

a $2500

b $6300

c $7100

d $10 900

2 The bank columns of a retailer's cash book showed a credit balance of $540. When the bank statement for the period was received it was necessary to make entries for the following items.

- Bank charges $40.
- Credit transfers received $280.
- Standing order payments $80.

What was the balance of the bank columns after updating the cash book?

a $140 credit

b $380 credit

c $700 credit

d $940 credit

3 Which one of the following items should be entered on the credit side of a sales ledger control account?

a Cash sales

b Discounts allowed

c Refunds to trade receivables

d Returns outwards

4 A purchases ledger control account contained the following items.

	$
Credit balance at beginning of period	4500
Credit purchases	5900
Interest charged on overdue accounts	200
Payments to trade payables	5400

What was the closing balance of the purchases ledger control account?

a $3800   **b** $4200   **c** $4800   **d** $5200

Shorter-Answer Questions: Bank Reconciliation

5 Prepare a bank reconciliation statement from the following information, clearly identifying the balance as per the bank statement.

	$
Debit balance per bank cash book	1898
Unpresented cheques	537
Uncredited deposits	914

6 Prepare a bank reconciliation statement from the following information, clearly identifying the balance as per the cash book.

	$
Credit balance per bank statement	259
Unpresented cheques	719
Uncredited deposits	672

7 Explain the difference between a direct debit and a standing order.

8 Explain **two** benefits to the owner of a business in preparing bank reconciliation statements regularly.

Shorter-Answer Questions: Control Accounts

9 A purchases ledger control account has been prepared which includes a debit balance. Give **one** reason why a purchases ledger account can have a debit balance.

10 Explain **three** benefits of preparing a sales ledger control account.

11 Which of the following items should be shown on the debit side of a purchases ledger control account?

cash purchases	payments to trade payables
credit purchases	refunds to trade payables
discounts received	returns inwards

12 Which of the following items should be shown on the debit side of a sales ledger control account?

- Irrecoverable debts written off
- Contra entry from sales ledger to purchases ledger
- Cheques received from trade receivables now dishonoured
- Credit sales
- Increase in provision for doubtful debts
- Receipts from trade receivables

Longer-Answer Questions: Bank Reconciliation Statements

13 *Comparing a cash book and bank statement, updating the cash book and preparing a bank reconciliation statement*

On 31 May 2018 the following bank statement was received by the accounts department of Raslinda Enterprises.

Premier Bank plc
Bank Statement for Raslinda Enterprises

Date		Details	Dr	Cr	Balance	
May	1	Balance			4880	Cr
	3	Sundry credit		850	5730	Cr
	8	723556 TDP Ltd	475		5255	Cr
	11	Credit transfer C Thomas		390	5645	Cr
	14	DD Regional Telecoms	220		5425	Cr
	18	723558 Hatford Ltd	188		5237	Cr
	20	Charges	54		5183	Cr
	25	723560 D Castle	293		4890	Cr
	26	Sundry credit		1370	6260	Cr

The business's cash book (bank columns) for May 2018 was as follows:

Dr			**Cash Book (bank columns only)**				Cr
May	1	Balance	4880	May	2	TDP Ltd (chq 723556)	475
	2	Cash sales	850		4	T Rajiv (chq 723557)	833
	23	L Aspen	820		8	Hatford Ltd (chq 723558)	188
	23	M Marco	550		19	Metro plc (chq 723559)	1380
	29	Cash sales	1230		22	D Castle (chq 723560)	293
					31	Balance c/d	5161
			8330				8330
June	1	Balance b/d	5161				

a Compare the cash book and bank statement for May 2018.

b Update the cash book at 31 May 2018.

c Prepare a bank reconciliation statement dated 31 May 2018.

> **GUIDANCE**
>
> Task **a** – When making the comparison it is a good idea to tick the items which appear in both documents as this helps isolate those items which will be required when answering tasks **b** and **c**.
>
> Task **b** – Remember you are adding items to the cash book which are currently only shown in the bank statement.
>
> Task **c** – The reconciliation statement makes use of those items currently shown in the cash book but missing from the bank statement.

14 *Updating the cash book and preparing a bank reconciliation statement working from a list of items including errors in the cash book or bank statement*

On 31 August 2018 Shamara compared her cash book (bank columns) and bank statement for the August. On this date her cash book showed a debit balance of $2382 and the bank statement showed a balance of $1268 credit. Shamara has identified the following differences between the two records.

- Bank charges of $84 which had been omitted from the cash book.
- A cheque sent to a supplier, MBM Ltd, $332 had not been presented for payment.
- A standing order for rent $485 had not been recorded in the cash book.
- The bank had not yet recorded cash sales of $1432 paid in on 29 August.
- The bank statement included a credit transfer of $441 from a customer, G Parsons, which had not been recorded in the cash book.
- A cheque for drawings $186 had been correctly recorded in the bank statement, but appears as $168 in the cash book.
- There was an error in the bank statement: some interest on Shamara's investments $132 had been credited to Shamara's business account rather than her personal account.

a Update the cash book at 31 August 2018.

b Prepare a bank reconciliation statement at 31 August 2018.

> **GUIDANCE**
>
> Don't forget to bring down the updated balance on the cash book and to give a full heading to the reconciliation statement which includes the date.

15 *Working with a bank overdraft*

Rockfort Stores is a retail business. The following cash book (bank columns) was prepared during the month of January 2018.

Dr			**Cash Book (bank columns only)**					Cr
Jan	1	Balance b/d	856	Jan	4	SO insurance	335
	10	Abbey Ltd	472		8	Tilt Ltd (chq 837441)	1578
	11	Mungroo Ltd	314		11	Samah Jones (chq 837442)	896
	23	Cash sales	471		15	DD water charges	540
	30	Cash sales	573		21	Hedrix plc (chq 837443)	1397
	31	Balance c/d	2360		26	Cash (chq 837444)	300
			5046				5046
				Feb	1	Balance b/d	2360

The business's bank statement for January 2018 was as follows.

Southern National Bank plc

Bank Statement for Rockfort Stores

Date		Details	Dr	Cr	Balance	
Jan	1	Balance			856	Cr
	4	SO Topmarks Insurance plc	335		521	Cr
	11	Chq 837441 Tilt Ltd	1578		1057	Dr
	15	Sundry credit		786	271	Dr
	15	DD Crystal Water Co Ltd	540		811	Dr
	17	Credit Transfer Helt plc		480	331	Dr
	26	Charges	139		470	Dr
	27	Chq 837442 Samah Jones	896		1366	Dr
	28	Sundry credit		471	895	Dr

a Explain why the standing order payment for insurance on 4 January is shown as a credit entry in the cash book but appears as a debit entry in the bank statement.

It has been noticed that an error was made in the cash book. The entry for cash sales on 30 January for $573 should have been for $375.

b Taking account of all the available information, update the bank columns of the cash book on 31 January 2018.

c What amount should be shown for the bank balance on Rockfort Stores' statement of financial position at 31 January 2018? State whether this amount should be shown as a current asset or a current liability.

d Prepare a bank reconciliation statement dated 31 January 2018.

> *GUIDANCE*
>
> *Check that negative figures are clearly identified by the use of brackets in the reconciliation statement.*

Longer-Answer Questions: Control Accounts

16 *Preparing control accounts for the sales ledger and the purchases ledger*

Henri regularly checks the accuracy of his business's sales and purchases ledger by preparing control accounts.

On 1 July 2018 the balances brought down on the two control accounts were:

	$
Purchases ledger control account	8 920
Sales ledger control account	11 430

On 31 July 2018 the following totals were extracted from the books of prime entry.

	$
Cash book: discounts allowed	880
Cash book: discounts received	472
Cash book: payments to trade payables	14 950
Cash book: receipts from trade receivables	22 748
Purchases journal	16 327
Sales return journal	491
Purchases returns journal	589
Sales journal	20 445

a Prepare a purchases ledger control account for July 2018.

b Prepare a sales ledger control account for July 2018.

> **GUIDANCE**
>
> *Before you prepare your answer, identify items which are relevant to trade payables for task **a** and those which are relevant to trade receivables for task **b**.*
>
> *When deciding where to make entries it is helpful to remember: a purchases ledger control account resembles a trade payables account; a sales ledger control account resembles a trade receivables account.*

17 *Preparing a sales ledger control account with more unusual entries and selecting relevant details*

Electra works in the accounts department of Horford Ltd. One of her duties is to prepare a sales ledger control account at the end of each month.

On 1 February 2018 the balances brought down on the sales ledger control account were: debit $23 786; credit $1034.

The following information for February 2018 has been extracted from the company's books of account.

	$
Irrecoverable debts written off	2 824
Cash sales	33 448
Cheques received from trade receivables but returned by the bank dishonoured	827
Contra entry (sales ledger account balances transferred to the purchases ledger)	440
Credit sales	85 492
Discounts allowed	3 721
Discounts received	2 240
Interest charged on overdue accounts of trade receivables	256
Receipts from trade receivables (including dishonoured cheques)	82 142
Refunds to trade receivables who overpaid their accounts	163
Returns from credit customers	3 462
Returns to credit suppliers	4 483

On 28 February 2018 there were credit balances totalling $620 in the sales ledger.

Prepare a sales ledger control account for February 2018 selecting relevant details from the available information.

> **GUIDANCE**
>
> *In this question there are some details which are not relevant to a sales ledger control account, so they must be ignored. Only items which would appear in an individual trade receivable's account can also appear in a sales ledger control account.*

18 *Preparing purchases and sales ledger control accounts including contra entries*

Andrew Bapniah makes use of control accounts to check the accuracy of his business's purchases and sales ledger.

On 1 June 2018 the balances brought down on the purchases ledger control account were: debit $414; credit $8450.

Andrew has provided the following information for June 2018.

	$
Contra entry (purchases ledger balance transferred to the sales ledger)	620
Credit purchases	23 726
Credit sales	40 185
Discounts allowed	382
Discounts received	561
Payments to trade payables	24 372
Receipts from trade receivables	38 993
Returns from credit customers	2 182
Returns to credit suppliers	1 927

On 30 June 2018 there was a debit balance in the purchases ledger of $225.

a Prepare a purchases ledger control account for June 2018.

The total of credit balances in the purchases ledger on 30 June 2018 was $4226.

b Explain what conclusions can be drawn from this information.

c Complete the following table indicating whether each of the following items should be shown in the sales ledger control account as a debit or credit entry. If the item should not be shown in the sales ledger control accounts write 'no entry'.

Item	Entry to be made in Sales Ledger Control Account
Credit sales	
Discounts allowed	
Returns outwards	
Contra entry (purchases ledger account balances transferred to the sales ledger)	

> **GUIDANCE**
>
> *In task **b** you should explain what it means if a control account closing balance does not agree with the figure for total receivables providing by the person responsible for preparing the sales ledger.*

Introduction

This section covers the preparation of financial statements for businesses with a single owner that are either trading or providing a service, i.e. income statements and statements of financial position. The shorter- and longer-answer units have been subdivided to cover:

- adjustments for other payables and other receivables
- depreciation and disposal of non-current assets
- bad debts and provisions for doubtful debts
- capital and revenue expenditure and receipts.

Multiple Choice Questions

1 The following information has been extracted from the books of a trader for a financial year.

	$
Carriage inwards	2 000
Inventory	
at beginning of period	17 000
at close of period	23 000
Purchases	56 000
Revenue	94 000

What was the trader's gross profit for the financial year?

a $30 000 **b** $32 000 **c** $42 000 **d** $44 000

2 The following figures have been extracted from a business's income statement.

	$
Inventory	
at beginning of period	30 000
at close of period	10 000
Purchases	200 000
Revenue	300 000

What is the business's cost of sales?

a $180 000 **b** $220 000 **c** $280 000 **d** $320 000

3 A business made a gross profit of $195 000 during a recent financial year. During the same period payments for expenses totalled $118 000. At the end of the financial year expenses accrued totalled $5000 and expenses prepaid totalled $10 000. What was the business's profit for the year?

a $62 000 **b** $67 000 **c** $82 000 **d** $92 000

4 The following information has been extracted from a business's books of account for the year ended 31 December 2018.

	$
Gross profit	123 000
Payments for expenses	76 000
Rent received	15 000

Expenses were prepaid $3000 and rent received was due $5000 at 31 December 2018.
What was the business's profit for the year?

a $54 000 **b** $60 000 **c** $64 000 **d** $70 000

5 A business uses the straight line method of depreciation. Recently a non-current asset was purchased for $10 000. This asset will be depreciated at a rate of 20% per annum.
What is the total provision for depreciation at the end of year 2?

a $1600 **b** $2000 **c** $3600 **d** $4000

6 A business owns a non-current asset which cost $80 000. The depreciation charge on this asset at the end of its second year was $15 000.
What was the business's depreciation policy?

a 20% per annum, reducing balance method

b 25% per annum, reducing balance method

c 20% per annum, straight line method

d 25% per annum, straight line method

7 A business made a draft profit of $47 800. However, it was discovered that an irrecoverable debt of $3000 should have been written off and a provision for doubtful debts of $2500 should have been made.
What will the business's amended profit be?

a $42 300 **b** $47 300 **c** $48 300 **d** $53 300

8 A business has trade receivables of $40 000. The policy is to maintain a provision for doubtful debts at 5% of trade receivables. The present provision for doubtful debts is $3500.
What double entry will be required in the general journal to update the provision for doubtful debts?

a Debit Income statement $1500   Credit Provision for doubtful debts $1500

b Debit Income statement $2000   Credit Provision for doubtful debts $2000

c Debit Provision for doubtful debts $1500   Credit Income statement $1500

d Debit Provision for doubtful debts $2000   Credit Income statement $2000

9 Which of the following should be treated as revenue expenditure in the accounts?

a Cost of adding logo to new delivery vehicle

b Installation of new computer system

c Repairs to roof of office building

d Wages of staff installing new computer system

10 Which of the following should be treated as a capital receipt in the accounts of a health and fitness centre?

a Fees paid by customers

b Interest received on bank account

c Loan from finance company

d Rent received from tenant

Shorter-Answer Questions: Adjustments for Other Payables and Other Receivables

11 At the end of a business's financial year the following amounts had been paid for each of these expenses.

	$
Administration expenses	3420
Insurance	1812
Interest on bank loan	740
Rent	9440

At the year end the following additional information is available.

- Administration expenses $270 is due but unpaid.
- Insurance includes $124 paid for the following year.
- Interest on the bank loan $50 is due but unpaid.
- Rent includes $620 paid for the following year.

Calculate the amount to be charged to the income statement prepared at the year end for each of the expenses.

12 The following items appeared in a business's trial balance at the end of the financial year, 31 December 2018.

	Dr	Cr
	$	$
Electricity charges	1930	
Interest received on loan		475
General expenses	626	
Rent received		5420

At the year end the following additional information is available.

- Electricity charges $210 are due but unpaid.
- Interest $110 is owed to the business.
- General expenses includes $90 paid for the following year.
- Rent received includes $240 received in advance.

a Calculate the amount to be charged to the income statement prepared at the year end for each of the listed items.

b List the items which should be shown as current assets in the business's statement of financial position at 31 December 2018.

c List the items which should be shown as current liabilities in the business's statement of financial position at 31 December 2018.

13 On 1 January 2018 a business owed $360 for water charges. During the year ended 31 December 2018 payments totalling $2730 were made for water charges. At 31 December 2018 the business owed $480 for water charges.

a Calculate the amount to be included for water charges in the income statement for the year ended 31 December 2018.

b Prepare the water charges account in the business's nominal ledger recording the information for 2018. Show the amount to be transferred to the income statement for the year ended 31 December 2018 and the closing balance brought down.

14 A business sublets part of its premises. On 1 January 2018 the tenant owed rent of $530. During the year ended 31 December 2018 the tenant paid a total of $6300 in rent. At 31 December 2018 the tenant had paid rent $490 in advance.

a Calculate the amount to be included for rent received in the business's income statement for the year ended 31 December 2018.

b Prepare the rent received account in the business's nominal ledger. Show the amount to be transferred to the income statement for the year ended 31 December 2018 and the closing balance brought down.

Shorter-Answer Questions: Depreciation and Disposal of Non-Current Assets

15 Yasmin uses the straight line method of depreciation. On 1 January 2018 she purchased new office equipment for $8400. She expects the office equipment to have a useful life of four years and to have a scrap value of $600 at the end of this time.

a Calculate the annual depreciation charge on the office equipment.

b Calculate the expected net book value of the office equipment at 31 December 2019.

c Prepare the provision for depreciation account for each of the years ended 31 December 2018 and 2019.

16 Ombeya uses the reducing balance method of depreciation. On 1 January 2018 he purchased a new motor vehicle for $18 000. He has decided to depreciate the motor vehicle at the rate of 20% per annum.

a Calculate the depreciation charge for the second year of ownership ending 31 December 2019.

b Calculate the expected net book value of the motor vehicle at 31 December 2019.

17 Mustafa owns a workshop where he repairs items of electrical equipment. The business's non-current assets include a collection of tools each of which has a low value. He uses the revaluation method to calculate the depreciation of these tools. On 1 January 2018 the tools were valued at $4750. During the year ended 31 December 2018 tools costing $890 were purchased. On 31 December 2018 the tools were revalued at $4620.

a Calculate the depreciation charge on the tools for the year ended 31 December 2018.

b Prepare the tools account in the business's nominal ledger for the year ended 31 December 2018. Show the amount to be transferred to the income statement for the year ended 31 December 2018 and the balance brought down.

18 Kalpna knows that many of her non-current assets are subject to wear and tear and that as a result she must calculate an annual depreciation charge on these assets. Give **three** other reasons for charging depreciation on non-current assets.

19 Raju recently sold some machinery which had cost $29 500. The machinery had been depreciated by $23 400 at the time of sale. The machinery was sold for $7200.

  a Calculate the profit or loss made on the disposal of the machinery.

  b Prepare the machinery disposal account as it should appear in the nominal ledger.

Shorter-Answer Questions: Irrecoverable Debts and Provisions for Doubtful Debts

20 On 31 December 2018 the owner of a business decided to create a provision for doubtful debts. On that date trade receivables totalled $17 200. The provision was to be 5% of trade receivables. What double-entry should be made to create the provision for doubtful debts?

21 A business maintains a provision for doubtful debts at 4% of trade receivables. On 1 January 2018 the provision amounted to $724. At 31 December 2018 trade receivables totalled $19 600. What double-entry is required to update the provision for doubtful debts?

22 A business maintains a provision for doubtful debts at 2% of trade receivables. On 1 January 2018 the provision amounted to $838. At 31 December 2018 trade receivables totalled $36 200.

  a What double-entry should be made to update the provision for doubtful debts?

  b What information about trade receivables should be shown in the business's statement of financial position at 31 December 2018?

Shorter-Answer Questions: Capital and Revenue Expenditure and Receipts

23 Explain what is meant by the terms:

  a capital expenditure

  b revenue expenditure

24 Explain what is meant by the terms:

  a capital receipts

  b revenue receipts

25 The owner of a business recently confused the terms revenue and capital receipts and recorded a loan from the business's bank as income in the income statement. Explain what effect this mistake will have on:

  a the calculation of profit for the year

  b the business's statement of financial position at the year end.

Longer-Answer Questions: Adjustments for Other Payables and Other Receivables; Depreciation and Disposal of Non-Current Assets

26 *Preparing financial statements including simple adjustments, depreciation with amounts given and goods for own use*

The following trial balance was extracted from the books of Andrew Nelson on 30 September 2018.

	Dr $	Cr $
Bank loan (repayable 2022)		8 000
Capital		77 100
Carriage inwards	620	
Bank	2 330	
Drawings	17 580	
Equipment		
cost	16 000	
provision for depreciation		4 000
General expenses	780	
Insurance	1 120	
Inventory at 1 October 2017	9 490	
Loan interest	730	
Premises		
cost	140 300	
provision for depreciation		14 030
Property taxes	650	
Purchases	49 440	
Rent received		2 290
Revenue		162 330
Trade payables		7 200
Trade receivables	4 800	
Wages	31 110	
	274 950	274 950

The following additional information is available at 30 September 2018.

- Inventory was valued at $3980.
- Andrew Nelson had taken goods value $240 for his own use but this had not yet been recorded in the accounts.
- Insurance includes $110 paid in advance.
- Depreciation of $3000 should be provided on the equipment, and $2806 on the premises.
- Rent received of $280 had been paid in advance by the tenant.
- Wages of $1200 is due but unpaid.

Prepare:

a an income statement for the year ended 30 September 2018

b a statement of financial position at 30 September 2018.

> **GUIDANCE**
>
> *Before you begin to write up your answer, look through the trial balance and identify items which are required for each part of the income statement and then for the statement of financial position. You may like to pencil in IS and SFP beside each item to help you. You should then work your way through each of the bullet points of additional information. Some of these require alterations to the amounts to be shown in the financial statements. You may like to pencil in the alterations beside the relevant items in the trial balance.*

27 *Preparing financial statements including simple adjustment, depreciation calculations and a loss on an asset disposal*

The following trial balance was extracted from the books of Speedy Supplies on 31 December 2018 after the calculation of the business's gross profit for the year ended on that date.

	Dr $	Cr $
Administration expenses	4 410	
Bank		1 710
Capital		223 000
Carriage outwards	820	
Drawings	21 770	
Furniture and equipment		
cost	20 000	
provision for depreciation		7 200
Gross profit		84 910
Insurance	1 680	
Inventory at 31 December 2018	17 450	
Loss on disposal of motor vehicle	430	
Premises		
cost	240 000	
provision for depreciation		19 200
Rent received		8 430
Trade payables		11 420
Trade receivables	14 450	
Wages and salaries	34 860	
	355 870	355 870

The following additional information is available at 31 December 2018.

- Administrative expenses $130 were due but unpaid.
- Insurance $480 was paid on 1 October 2018; this amount gives cover for six months ended 31 March 2019.
- Depreciation should be provided on the furniture and equipment at 20% per annum using the reducing balance method; depreciation should be provided on the premises at 2% per annum using the straight line method.
- The premises are sublet and one tenant owes rent of $390; a second tenant has paid rent in advance of $820.
- Wages and salaries of $730 are due but unpaid.

Prepare:

a an income statement for the year ended 31 December 2018

b a statement of financial position at 31 December 2018.

> **GUIDANCE**
>
> *Do not forget to give each financial statement a full and correct heading avoiding abbreviations and show workings for the calculations you make.*

Longer-Answer Questions: Irrecoverable Debts and Provisions for Doubtful Debts

28 *Preparing an income statement including Irrecoverable debts and the creation of a provision for doubtful debts as well as other adjustments*

A sole trader prepared a trial balance at the end of the business's financial year, 31 August 2018. The trial balance included the following information:

	Dr	Cr
	$	$
Debts written off recovered		120
Irrecoverable debts	494	
Carriage inwards	272	
Carriage outwards	119	
Discounts	327	448
Electricity	1 873	
General expenses	1 020	
Interest received		392
Inventory, 1 September 2017	4 847	
Purchases	49 371	
Rent	12 392	
Returns	827	238
Revenue		106 481
Trade receivables	12 400	
Vehicles		
cost	21 200	
provision for depreciation		5 300
Wages	12 272	
Water charges	994	

The following additional information is available at 31 August 2018.

- Inventory was valued at $3922.
- Electricity charges $189 were due but unpaid.
- Interest of $120 was due but not yet received.
- Water charges included $116 paid in advance.
- Depreciation should be provided on the vehicles at 25% per annum using the straight line method.
- It was decided that a provision for doubtful debts should be created at 4% of trade receivables.

Prepare an income statement for the year ended 31 August 2018.

GUIDANCE

The question includes discounts and returns. These are shown deliberately in such a way as to leave it to you to decide which are discounts allowed and which discounts received, and which are sales returns and purchases returns. This presentation can cause confusion. To help you distinguish remember that discounts allowed is an expense and discounts received is income; in the case of returns inwards remember this is set against revenue, and returns outwards is set against purchases.

---

29 *Preparing financial statements including a change to the provision for doubtful debts*

Avonford Traders is a wholesale business. Its most recent financial year ended on 31 December 2018. On that date the following trial balance was extracted.

	Dr	Cr
	$	$
Advertising	3 400	
Bank loan (repayable 2022)		12 500
Bank loan interest	940	
Capital		65 000
Bank	7 250	
Discounts received		370
Drawings	32 410	
Furniture and equipment		
cost	17 800	
provision for depreciation		8 400
Insurance	2 230	
Inventory, 1 January 2018	27 650	
Motor vehicles		
cost	36 000	
provision for depreciation		12 960
Profit on disposal of furniture		240
Provision for doubtful debts, 1 January 2018		640
Purchases	82 980	
Rent	11 480	
Revenue		174 360
Trade payables		9 970
Trade receivables	18 200	
Wages	44 100	
	284 440	284 440

The following additional information is available at 31 December 2018.
- Inventory was valued at $31 350.
- Advertising included $480 paid in advance.
- Wages $1820 was due but unpaid.
- Depreciation should be provided on furniture and equipment at 15% on cost; depreciation should be provided on motor vehicles at 20% per annum using the reducing balance method.
- The provision for doubtful debts was maintained at 4% of trade receivables.

Prepare:

a an income statement for the year ended 31 December 2018

b a statement of financial position at 31 December 2018.

> GUIDANCE
>
> This question includes the updating of the provision for doubtful debts. It is important to remember that only the change in the provision is recorded in the income statement. It may be helpful to think of any increase in the provision as requiring more profit to be taken out of circulation, and any decrease in the provision as requiring less profit to be taken out of circulation.

Longer-Answer Questions: Capital and Revenue Expenditure and Receipts

30 *Identifying capital and revenue expenditure and receipts and explaining why it is important to distinguish between the terms*

Leon owns a business called 'Island Tours'. The business provides coach trips and holidays. During the year ended 30 September 2018 the following transaction occurred.

Transaction	Revenue expenditure	Capital expenditure	Revenue receipt	Capital receipt
Paid wages of coach drivers				
Sold coach which was at end of its useful life				
Took out a bank loan				
Paid for repairs to a coach				
Amounts received from customers for coach trips				
Paid for extension to garage buildings				
Paid interest on bank loan				
Leon paid some of his private funds into the business				
Purchased new coach				
Paid to have business logo added to new coach				

a Identify each item as one of: revenue expenditure, capital expenditure, revenue receipt or capital receipt. Place a tick (✔) in the appropriate column.

b Explain why it is important to distinguish correctly between these different types of transaction.

> GUIDANCE
>
> In part **b** you should aim to show how well you understand these types of transaction by referring to the effects of making mistakes in identification when preparing income statements and statements of financial position. Providing examples can help show you really understand this topic.

31 *Preparing financial statements for a service business including an intangible asset and the correct treatment of capital and revenue expenditure as well as other adjustments*

Kisha owns Premier Car Hire. Her business's financial year ended on 31 October 2018 when the following trial balance was prepared.

	Dr	Cr
	$	$
Irrecoverable debt	120	
Capital		300 000
Bank	8 210	
Drawings	31 330	
Furniture and equipment		
cost	6 300	
provision for depreciation		1 260
Goodwill	30 000	
Insurance	8 320	
Motor vehicle running costs	11 490	
Motor vehicles		
cost	95 000	
provision for depreciation		19 000
Motor vehicles repairs	3 940	
Office expenses	840	
Premises		
cost	230 000	
provision for depreciation		6 900
Provision for doubtful debts		210
Rent receivable		1 850
Revenue		125 610
Trade payables		880
Trade receivables	4 800	
Wages and salaries	25 360	
	455 710	455 710

The following additional information is available at 31 October 2018.

- Office expenses $140 was due but unpaid.
- Insurance includes $190 paid in advance.
- Rent $290 has been received in advance.
- The provision for doubtful debts is to be reduced to $140.
- Depreciation is to be provided on non-current assets as follows: premises $6900; furniture and equipment 20% per annum on cost; motor vehicles 20% per annum using the reducing balance method.
- At the end of October 2018 air-conditioning was installed in the business's premises at a cost of $9000. On 31 October 2018 a cheque for $9000 was sent to the installer. However, this transaction has not yet been recorded in the business's books of account.

Prepare:

a an income statement for the year ended 31 October 2018

b a statement of financial position at 31 October 2018.

Introduction

In this section there are questions to test your understanding of the preparation of the financial statements of partnerships including the use of separate current and capital accounts. You will also test your understanding of the background knowledge relating to partnerships: advantages, disadvantages of forming a partnership, purpose of partnership agreements and the function of key financial statements.

Multiple Choice Questions

1 Pat and Rob are in partnership sharing profits and losses in the ratio 4:3 respectively. The partnership has just made a profit of $105 000. Which entry should be made in Rob's current account?

   a   Credit $45 000   **b**   Credit $60 000

   c   Debit $45 000   **d**   Credit $60 000

2 Which of the following should be credited to a partner's current account?

   a   Drawings   **b**   Interest on capital

   c   Interest on drawings   **d**   Share of loss

3 Shazeem and Tariq are in partnership sharing profits and losses equally. The partnership agreement provides for Tariq to receive a partnership salary of $10 000 per annum. The partnership made a loss before appropriation of $32 000 during the year ended 31 December 2018.

   What is Tariq's net share of the loss for the year ended 31 December 2018?

   a $6000   **b** $11 000   **c** $16 000   **d** $21 000

4 Rachel and Seema are in partnership sharing profits and losses equally after charging interest on drawings. During the year ended 30 September 2018, the partnership made a profit before appropriation of $80 000. Interest on drawings for the year ended 30 September 2018 was: Rachel $5000, Seema $3000.

   What was Rachel's net share of the profits for the year?

   a $31 000   **b** $39 000   **c** $41 000   **d** $49 000

Shorter-Answer Questions

5 Which of the following items should be included in a partnership appropriation account?

   drawings   interest on a partner's loan

   interest on capital   partnership salary

   interest on drawings   share of loss

6 Which of the following should be included in a partner's current account on the debit side, and which should be shown on the credit side?

   drawings   interest on a partner's loan

   interest on capital   partnership salary

   interest on drawings   share of loss

7 Salma and Tony are considering forming a partnership. They realise that they will have more capital available as a result of forming the partnership, but that they will have unlimited liability for the debts of the business.

   a State **two** other advantages that may arise from forming the partnership.

   b State **one** other disadvantage that may arise from forming the partnership.

8 Rudy and Sherelle prepared a deed of partnership when they formed a partnership, setting out the rules under which they would work together. The agreement included the ratio in which they would share profits. List **four** other matters that you would expect the partners to have included in the deed of partnership.

9 Pamela and Robin are in partnership sharing profits and losses in the ratio 4:5 respectively. Their partnership agreement also provides for Pamela to receive a salary of $15 000 per annum for managing the business. Partners are also entitled to interest on fixed capitals at 10% per annum. The partners' capital account balances are: Pamela $80 000, Robin $110 000. During the year ended 31 August 2018 the partnership made a profit of $133 000.

   a Calculate Pamela's total share of the profits for the year ended 31 August 2018.

   b Calculate Robin's total share of the profits for the year ended 31 August 2018.

10 Ahmed and Bamber are in partnership sharing profits and losses in the ratio 3:2 respectively after charging interest on drawings and providing Bamber with a salary of $22 000 per annum. During the year ended 31 October 2018 interest on drawings amounted to: Ahmed $2000, Bamber $3000. The partnership made a loss before appropriation of $39 000 during the year ended 31 October 2018.

   a Calculate Ahmed's net share of the loss for the year ended 31 October 2018.

   b Calculate Bamber's net share of the loss for the year ended 31 October 2018.

Longer-Answer Questions

11 *Preparing an appropriation account to share out a profit, including interest on capital and a partnership salary*

Emilie and Marco are in partnership sharing profits and losses in the ratio 3:2. Their partnership agreement includes the following.

- The partners are to make capital contributions which are fixed at: Emilie $80 000; Marco $50 000.
- Emilie is to receive a partnership salary of $8000 per annum.
- Partners are entitled to interest on capital at 8% per annum.

During the year ended 30 November 2018, the partnership made a profit of $74 000.

Prepare an appropriation account for the year ended 30 November 2018.

> *GUIDANCE*
>
> *Calculate each partner's interest on capital first and include your workings as part of your answer. Give the appropriation account a full title. Remember to start with the total profit and deduct each of the appropriations from this amount.*

12 *Preparing partners' current accounts*

Rakesh and Vikash are in partnership sharing profits and losses equally. On 1 January 2018 the balances of their current accounts were:

Rakesh $4500 debit

Vikash $6200 credit

The partnership made a profit of $38 600 during the year ended 31 December 2018. This was shared in accordance with the partnership agreement as follows:

- Interest on drawings: Rakesh $640; Vikash $820.
- Partnership salary of $18 000 for Rakesh.
- Interest on capital: Rakesh $8200; Vikash $7400.
- During the year ended 31 December 2018 the partners' drawings were: Rakesh $16 000; Vikash $20 500.

a Calculate each partner's share of the residual profit.

b Prepare the partners' current accounts. Balance the accounts at 31 December 2018.

c State what the closing balance of each partner's current account represents.

> **GUIDANCE**
>
> *It is a good idea to prepare one account with separate columns for each partner as this saves time. Don't forget to bring down the closing balances on the partners' current accounts. Balances must always have a correct narrative, i.e. balance b/d, balance c/d. As task* **b** *requires accounts, it would not be acceptable to present a calculation or vertical list of entries which contain a mix of positive and negative items.*

13 *Preparing a partnership's statement of financial position*

Amanda and Sylvia are in partnership sharing profits and losses equally after allowing interest on the partners' fixed capitals at the rate of 10% per annum.

At 31 December 2018, the following balances appeared in the books of the partnership **before the appropriation of profits** for the year ended on that date and the preparation of a statement of financial position at 31 December 2018.

	$	
Capital accounts		
Amanda	60 000	
Sylvia	50 000	
Bank	3 200	
Current accounts, 1 January 2018		
Amanda	600	debit
Sylvia	2 500	credit
Drawings		
Amanda	21 200	
Sylvia	26 500	
Inventory	14 200	
Non-current assets at net book value	87 300	
Other payables	600	
Other receivables	700	
Profit for the year	42 400	
Trade payables	6 500	
Trade receivables	8 300	

a Calculate each partner's share of the profit for the year ended 31 December 2018.

b Prepare the partnership's statement of financial position at 31 December 2018. The statement should include detailed current accounts.

GUIDANCE

Provide detailed workings of each partner's profit share, as this information will be required when setting out the current accounts within the statement of financial position. Ensure that capital account and current account information is kept quite separate within the statement of financial position. Don't forget to show any negative figures in the current account detail in brackets.

---

14 *Preparing a partnership's income statement and appropriation account including interest on a partner's loan and a more complex profit-sharing agreement*

Kalpa and Samir are in partnership sharing profits and losses equally. Their partnership agreement includes the following terms:

- Samir is entitled to receive interest on his loan at 5% per annum.
- Interest on total drawings should be charged at 10% per annum.
- Each partner should receive interest on fixed capitals at 8% per annum.
- Kalpa should receive an annual salary of $15 000.

The following information has been extracted from the partnership's books of account for the year ended 30 September 2018.

	$
Administration expenses	3 640
Capital accounts	
Kalpa	90 000
Samir	70 000
Carriage outwards	1 430
Drawings	
Kalpa	23 200
Samir	17 800
Furniture and equipment	
at cost	50 000
provision for depreciation, 1 October 2017	18 000
Insurance	3 410
Inventory, 1 October 2017	14 440
Loan from Samir	18 000
Purchases	83 450
Sales returns	830
Revenue	139 910
Wages	29 620

Additional information:

- Inventory at 30 September 2018 was valued at $11 250.
- Insurance, $290, was prepaid at 30 September 2018.
- Wages due but unpaid totalled $430 at 30 September 2018.
- Depreciation should be provided on furniture and equipment at the rate of 20% per annum using the reducing balance method.

Prepare:

a an income statement for the year ended 30 September 2018

b an appropriation account for the year ended 30 September 2018.

GUIDANCE

Do not forget to present the financial statements with full titles and to show workings for adjustments and other calculations.

Introduction

In this section there are questions to test your understanding of the preparation of the financial statements of limited liability companies. You will also test your knowledge of how a limited company is financed through the issue of share capital and how shareholders are rewarded by the payment of dividends.

Multiple Choice Questions

1 Which statement best describes the authorised share capital of a limited company?

  a The total value of the called-up share capital.

  b The total value of the paid-up share capital.

  c The total value of the share capital that a limited company is permitted to issue.

  d The total value of the share capital that shareholders have purchased.

2 Which statement best describes the called-up share capital of a limited company?

  a The number of shares that have been partly paid.

  b The number of shares that have been requested to be paid by the company.

  c The value of share capital that has been requested to be paid by the company.

  d The value of share capital that has been partly paid.

3 Which one of the following will not appear in the statement of changes in equity of a limited company?

  a Loss for the year

  b Ordinary share dividends paid

  c Ordinary share dividends proposed

  d Profit for the year

4 A limited company has an authorised share capital of 400 000 ordinary shares of 50c each, all of which have been called-up. The directors required the payment of 30c per share and on 1 July 2018, 80% of this sum had been received. What is the paid-up share capital of the company at 1 July 2018?

  a $96 000

  b $120 000

  c $200 000

  d $240 000

Shorter-Answer Questions

5 Explain briefly the difference between:

  a the shareholders of a limited company and the directors of a limited company

  b ordinary shares and preference shares.

6 Explain how the following would arise in the financial statements of a limited company.

  a retained earnings

  b general reserve

7 The authorised share capital of A Ltd is 300 000 ordinary shares of $0.25 each. The issued share capital of the company is 50 000 ordinary shares of $0.25 each. The directors have announced a dividend of 5%.

Calculate the value of the ordinary share dividend.

8 The authorised share capital of O Limited is as follows:

8% preference shares of $1 each	$200 000
500 000 ordinary shares of $0.50 each	$250 000

The company has issued 80 000 of the 8% preference shares and the issued ordinary share capital totals $150 000.

The directors have declared an ordinary share dividend of $0.05 per ordinary share and will pay the preference share dividend in full.

Calculate the full amount of dividends to be paid for each class of shares.

9 B Ltd has authorised share capital consisting of 600 000 ordinary shares of 50c each and 200 000 6% preference shares of $1 each. All of the preference shares had been issued and were fully paid up. 400 000 of the ordinary shares had been issued and 30c per share had been called up and paid.

The directors have declared an ordinary share dividend of 5% and will pay the preference share dividend in full.

Calculate the full amount of dividends to be paid for each class of share.

Longer-Answer Questions

10 *Preparing the income statement for a limited company*

The following information has been taken from the books of R Ltd at the end of its financial year, 30 November 2018.

	$
10% debentures 2026	40 000
Business expenses	84 000
Debenture interest	4 000
Directors' salaries	66 000
Inventory at 1 December 2017	93 000
Issued share capital	
150 000 ordinary shares of $1 each fully paid	150 000
50 000 6% preference shares of $1 each fully paid	50 000
Non-current assets	
Cost	520 000
Provision for depreciation at 1 December 2017	240 000
Purchases	365 000
Revenue	842 000

Additional information:

- Inventory at 30 November 2018 was valued at $106 000.
- Depreciation should be provided on non-current assets at 20% using the reducing balance method.
- Business expenses prepaid at 30 November 2018 were $3000.
- The directors wish to pay a full year's dividend on the preference shares.

Prepare an income statement for the year ended 30 November 2018.

> **GUIDANCE**
>
> *Remember that the income statement should show a gross profit for the year before any expenses are deducted. Expenses should include all depreciation of non-current assets. The income statement should also show an operating profit for the year, i.e. the profit before any interest charges are deducted. Don't forget that interest charges include not only debenture interest but preference share dividends as well. The statement ends with the profit or loss for the year. It is a common error to forget to label these important subtotals.*

11 *Preparing the income statement for a limited company*

The following information has been taken from the books of S Ltd at the end of its financial year, 30 September 2018.

	$
5% debentures 2026	54 000
Business expenses	152 250
Debenture interest	2 025
Directors' salaries	48 500
Inventory at 1 October 2017	62 000
Issued share capital	
200 000 ordinary shares of 25c each fully paid	50 000
80 000 6% preference shares of $1 each fully paid	80 000
Non-current assets	
Cost	80 000
Provision for depreciation at 1 October 2017	48 000
Preference share dividends paid	2 400
Purchases	285 000
Revenue	615 000

Additional information:

- Inventory at 30 September 2018 was valued at $59 000.
- Debenture interest has been paid up to 30 June 2018.
- The directors wish to provide for the outstanding part of the preference share dividend at 30 September 2018.
- Depreciation should be provided on non-current assets at 15% using the straight line method
- Business expenses prepaid at 30 September 2018 were $3250.
- Business expenses accrued at 30 September 2018 were $1600.

Prepare an income statement for the year ended 30 September 2018.

GUIDANCE

Remember to show clearly labels for gross profit for the year, operating profit and profit for the year. Debenture interest and the preference share dividend have both been part paid during the year. Depreciation should all be charged to business expenses. Remember to include the name of the company in your answer and to give a full heading for the income statement avoiding any abbreviations.

12 *Preparing the statement of changes in equity*

The following is an extract from B Ltd's statement of financial position at 30 June 2018.

	$
Equity	
Share capital and reserves	
Ordinary shares of $1 each fully paid	150 000
General reserve	26 000
Retained earnings	146 000
	322 000

- The profit for the year ended 30 June 2018 was $85 000.
- The directors paid an ordinary share dividend of 12c per share during the year.
- The directors wish to transfer $40 000 to the general reserve.

Prepare a statement of changes in equity for the year ended 30 June 2018.

GUIDANCE

Prepare your statement of changes in equity using four columns – ordinary share capital, retained earnings, general reserve and total. Remember that the profit for the year will increase the balance of retained earnings and that the ordinary share dividends paid and the transfer to general reserve will decrease the balance of retained earnings.

13 *Preparing the statement of changes in equity*

The following is an extract from S Ltd's statement of financial position at 30 September 2018.

	$
Equity	
Share capital and reserves	
Ordinary shares of 50c each fully paid	125 000
General reserve	60 000
Retained earnings	12 000
	197 000

- The profit for the year ended 30 September 2018 was $62 000.
- The directors paid an ordinary share dividend of 15c per share during the year.
- The directors wish to transfer $20 000 to the general reserve.

Prepare a statement of changes in equity for the year ended 30 September 2018.

(See page 58 for Guidance)

> *GUIDANCE*
>
> *Note that the ordinary shares are in units of 50c each, so take care with your calculation of the number of shares issued by this company.*

14 *Preparing the statement of financial position for a limited company*
has an authorised share capital as follows:

6% preference shares of $1 each	$300 000
400 000 ordinary shares of $1 each	$400 000

The following information was available at 30 June 2018.

	$
6% debentures (2026)	40 000
Bank	14 900
Inventories	63 500
Issued share capital	
6% preference shares of $1 each fully paid	150 000
200 000 ordinary shares of $1 each fully paid	200 000
Non-current assets at cost	465 000
Non-current assets provision for depreciation	102 400
Other payables	1 200
Other receivables	3 200
Retained earnings	65 400
Trade payables	14 600
Trade receivables	27 000

Prepare a statement of financial position at 30 June 2018.

> *GUIDANCE*
>
> *Remember that it is the issued share capital that appears in the statement of financial position, not the authorised share capital. Ordinary shares should precede preference shares in the list of issued capital.*

15 *Preparing the statement of financial position for a limited company*

S Ltd has an authorised share capital as follows:

5% preference shares of $1 each	$200 000
500 000 ordinary shares of 50c each	$250 000

The following information was available at 31 March 2018.

	$
8% debentures (2023)	20 000
Bank	2 900
Inventories	42 300
Issued share capital	
5% preference shares of $1 each fully paid	90 000
240 000 ordinary shares of 50c each fully paid	120 000
Non-current assets at cost	316 000
Non-current assets provision for depreciation	122 600
Other payables	1 600
Other receivables	5 800
Provision for doubtful debts	900
Retained earnings	21 900
Trade payables	22 400
Trade receivables	38 200

Prepare a statement of financial position at 31 March 2018.

GUIDANCE

Trade receivables should be shown after the provision for doubtful debts has been deducted.

---

16 *Preparing the income statement, statement of changes in equity and statement of financial position for a limited company*

M Ltd has an authorised share capital as follows:

6% preference shares of $1 each	$150 000
600 000 ordinary shares of $1 each	$600 000

The following trial balance has been extracted at 31 July 2018:

	Dr $	Cr $
Business expenses	115 300	
Bank	8 900	
Directors' salaries	48 000	
General reserve		22 000
Inventory at 1 August 2017	42 800	
Issued share capital		
6% preference shares of $1 each fully paid		80 000
200 000 ordinary shares of $1 each fully paid		200 000
Non-current assets at cost	375 000	
Non-current assets provision for depreciation		63 000
Ordinary share dividends paid	12 000	
Other payables		1 100
Other receivables	4 700	
Preference share dividend paid	2 400	
Provision for doubtful debts		600
Purchases	212 600	
Retained earnings		29 000
Revenue		448 200
Trade payables		16 900
Trade receivables	39 100	
	860 800	860 800

Additional information:
- Inventory at 31 July 2018 was valued at $49 200.
- Preference share dividend of $2400 is still owing at 31 July 2018.
- The provision for doubtful debts is to be increased by $300 at 31 July 2018.
- Business expenses of $4500 have been paid in advance at 31 July 2018

Prepare the following:

a an income statement for the year ended 31 July 2018

b a statement of changes in equity for the year ended 31 July 2018

c a statement of financial position at 31 July 2018.

GUIDANCE

This question brings together the three parts of the financial statements of a limited company. Take each statement in turn and remember that the inventory shown in the trial balance is the opening inventory to appear in the income statement, not the closing inventory.

---

17 *Preparing the income statement, statement of changes in equity and statement of financial position for a limited company*

R Ltd has an authorised share capital as follows:

5% preference shares of $1 each	$220 000
900 000 ordinary shares of 50c each	$450 000

The following balances have been extracted at 30 April 2018.

	$
Bank	11 200
Business expenses	185 700
Directors' salaries	62 000
General reserve	30 000
Inventory at 1 May 2017	53 000
Issued share capital	
5% preference shares of $1 each fully paid	140 000
500 000 ordinary shares of 50c each fully paid	250 000
Non-current assets at cost	632 000
Non-current assets provision for depreciation	140 000
Ordinary share dividends paid	25 000
Other payables	3 000
Other receivables	2 200
Preference share dividend paid	3 500
Provision for doubtful debts	1 500
Purchases	324 000
Retained earnings	106 500
Revenue	638 100
Trade payables	39 900
Trade receivables	72 800

Additional information:
- Inventory at 30 April 2018 was valued at $61 000.
- Preference share dividend of $3500 is still owing at 30 April 2018.
- The provision for doubtful debts is to be reduced by $200 at 30 April 2018.
- Business expenses of $6000 have been paid in advance at 30 April 2018

Prepare the following:

a An income statement for the year ended 30 April 2018.

b A statement of changes in equity for the year ended 30 April 2018.

c A statement of financial position at 30 April 2018.

> *GUIDANCE*
>
> *You may find it helpful to mark up each listed item as to whether it will appear in the income statement (I) or statement of changes in equity (E) or statement of financial position (P). You might also like to pencil in any changes to the figures which result from information given in additional information.*

Introduction

This section has a range of questions to test your knowledge and understanding of the preparation of financial statements of clubs and societies. You will have the opportunity to focus on the main techniques which are required in order to be successful in preparing these statements, including:

- distinguishing between receipts and payments and income and expenditure accounts
- preparing receipts and payments accounts
- preparing accounts for revenue generating activities
- preparing income and expenditure accounts
- preparing a club's statement of financial position
- making adjustments including those for members' subscriptions
- calculating the accumulated fund.

The financial statements of clubs are prepared on the same basis as that of a business. However, as a club is a non-profit making organisation, the accounts prepared and the terminology used are different. Large clubs keep a full set of books, but smaller clubs prepare their financial statements on a single-entry basis.

The club's treasurer prepares an annual summary of the bank and cash transactions in a receipts and payments account. Although they are non-profit making organisations, some clubs run profit-making activities such as refreshments or a shop. This requires a separate account to be prepared.

The main source of income is the subscriptions from members. Most clubs also have other fund-raising activities.

The main account is the income and expenditure account, which is similar to an income statement, and is prepared on an accruals basis. The balance on this account is either a surplus or a deficit.

A statement of financial position is prepared showing the club's assets and liabilities. The capital account is replaced with an accumulated fund.

Multiple Choice Questions

1 What is the definition of the term accumulated fund?

  a It is the capital account.

  b It is the members' donations.

  c It is the total assets owned by the club.

  d It is the total of the club's surpluses over a period of years.

2 A credit balance on the income and expenditure account is described as:

  a excess income

  b profit for the year

  c profit on trading

  d surplus income over expenditure.

3 During 2018 a club received $3200 in subscriptions from its members. Of these $240 was in advance for 2019. Subscriptions of $120 were in arrears for 2018.

What was the income for subscriptions for 2018?

a $2960

b $3080

c $3320

d $3440

4 At the beginning of 2018 a club had subscriptions in arrears of $96 and in advance of $58. During the year subscriptions of $2950 were received in cash. At the end of the year subscriptions of $70 were paid in advance and $120 were in arrears.

What was the income for subscriptions for 2018?

a $2862

b $2962

c $3038

d $3178

5 A club received a donation which had to be treated as capital revenue. How should the donation appear in the financial statements?

a A long-term liability in the statement of financial position.

b Added to the accumulated fund in the statement of financial position.

c Deducted from the accumulated fund in the statement of financial position.

d Income in the income and expenditure account.

6 At the beginning of 2018 a club owed suppliers $420 for supplies of refreshments. During the year it purchased $4650 of goods, and owed $360 at the end of the year.

What were the purchases for the year?

a $4590 b $4650 c $4710 d $5430

Shorter-Answer Questions

7 At 1 April 2018 the Hatton Social Club had the following assets and liabilities.

	$
Bank	650
Equipment	7 200
Fixtures and fittings	2 320
Inventory	420
Amounts due to suppliers	270
Subscriptions in advance	140
Subscriptions in arrears	190
Loans from members	2 500

Prepare a statement of affairs to calculate the accumulated fund.

8 The Socco Football Club's annual subscription is $25.

At 1 January 2018 there were subscriptions in arrears of $150 and in advance of $75.

During the year the subscriptions received in cash were $3600. Included in this were subscriptions in advance for 2019 for four members. At 31 December 2018 subscriptions were in arrears from eight members.

a Prepare the subscriptions account showing the amount to be transferred to the income and expenditure account.

b Show the entry for subscriptions in the income and expenditure account.

9 Prepare a profit-making account, with inventory and trade payables

The Greenpath Gardening Club has a shop which provides members with seeds, plants and gardening equipment.

Information for the shop for the year ended 31 March 2018 was:

	$
Opening inventory	1 500
Closing inventory	1 800
Payments to trade payables for inventory	16 300
Sales revenue	22 000
Trade payables for inventory 1 April 2017	300
Trade payables for inventory 31 March 2018	450
Wages for casual labour	2 200
Shop expenses	540

a Prepare the shop account for the year ended 31 March 2018.

b Show the entry for the shop profit or loss in the income and expenditure account for the year ended 31 March 2018.

10 At 1 April 2017 the Pastures Sports Club had a positive balance of cash and cash equivalents of $810.

A summary of the club's receipts for the year was:

	$
Subscriptions	4250
Competition fees	560
Bank loan	1000
Sale of refreshments	2800

A summary of the club's payments was:

	$
Purchase of equipment	3200
Competition prizes	400
Purchase of refreshments	1850
Maintenance of ground	2300
Insurance	450
General expenses	740

Prepare the club's receipts and payments account for the year ended 31 March 2018.

Longer-Answer Questions

11 *Preparing an income and expenditure account and statement of financial position*
The following information relates to the Trent Fishing Club.

Assets and liabilities at	1 January 2018	31 December 2018
	$	$
Clubhouse	15 000	14 500
Equipment	4 200	?
Loans from members	2 000	2 800
General expenses accrued	250	300
Insurance prepaid	440	490
Subscriptions in arrears	125	250
Subscriptions in advance	85	40
Accumulated fund	18 780	?

Dr		Receipts and Payments Account for the year ended 31 December 2018		Cr
	$		$
Balance b/d	1 350	Purchases of refreshments	1 100
Subscriptions	12 500	General expenses	3 730
Sales of refreshments	1 630	Insurance	2 200
Donation	400	Equipment	3 800
Loans from members	800	Secretary's expenses	1 620
		Balance c/d	4 230
	16 680		16 680

Additional information:

- Equipment had to be depreciated at 10% per annum straight line method on the closing balance.
- The donation had to be treated as capital revenue and had to be credited to the accumulated fund.

Prepare:

a the subscriptions account for the year

b the income and expenditure account for the year ended 31 December 2018

c a statement of financial position at 31 December 2018.

> *GUIDANCE*
>
> *Remember to include the opening balance of cash and cash equivalents in the opening statement of affairs.*
>
> *Note the difference between the opening and closing clubhouse balance is depreciation.*
>
> *As there is no inventory or amounts owing for refreshments, all that is required in the income and expenditure account is to net off the sales and purchases of refreshments, and include the net income in the income section.*

12 *Preparing an income and expenditure account and statement of financial position*

The following information relates to the Bromley Tennis Club for the year ended 31 December 2018.

Balances at	1 January 2018	31 December 2018
	$	$
Subscriptions in advance	85	105
Subscriptions in arrears	240	180
Equipment	10 500	?
Inventory of refreshments	180	220
Trade payables for refreshments	300	200

Dr	Receipts and Payments Account for the year ended 31 December 2018		Cr
	$		$
Balance b/d	2 100	Purchases of refreshments	2 300
Subscriptions received	28 500	Wages	18 000
Tennis court hire fees	3 600	Insurance	2 025
Sale of refreshments	5 550	Tennis court maintenance	3 860
Donation	800	General expenses	820
		Equipment	9 500
		Balance c/d	4 045
	40 550		40 550

Additional information at 31 December 2018:

- Equipment had to be depreciated at 10% per annum straight line. Of the total depreciation for the year, 25% relates to refreshments.
- Included in the wages is $1000 relating to refreshments.
- Insurance is prepaid $225.
- General expenses accrued $80.
- The donation had to be treated as revenue income.

Prepare:

a a statement of affairs to calculate the opening accumulated fund

b the refreshments account

c the subscriptions account

d an income and expenditure account for the year ended 31 December 2018

e a statement of financial position at 31 December 2018.

> *GUIDANCE*
>
> *Remember to include the balance of cash and cash equivalents in the opening statement of affairs, and in the closing statement of financial position. Calculate the total depreciation for the year, then allocate 25% to the refreshments account as an expense deducted from the gross profit, and 75% to the income and expenditure account as an expense. In the income and expenditure account net off the tennis court fees against the cost of maintenance. As the costs are higher than the fees, the difference will be included in the expenditure. The donation should be included in the income section of the income and expenditure account as it is described as revenue income.*

Introduction

In this section there are questions to test your understanding of the preparation of a manufacturing account. You will also test your knowledge of the preparation of an income statement and a statement of financial position for a manufacturing business.

Multiple Choice Questions

1 Which one of the following factory costs is a direct cost?

a Factory rent

b Machine depreciation

c Machine operators' wages

d Maintenance costs

2 Which one of the following will appear in a manufacturing account?

a Closing inventory of finished goods

b Closing work in progress

c Depreciation of office equipment

d Purchase of finished goods

3 What is prime cost?

a Total direct material cost

b Total direct material and direct labour costs

c Total direct material, direct labour and other indirect expenses costs

d Total of all manufacturing overheads

4 Which one of the following is part of prime cost?

a Carriage inwards

b Indirect wages

c Machine depreciation

d Supervisor's salary

Shorter-Answer Questions

5 Explain why a manufacturing business produces a manufacturing account.

6 Explain why adjustments are made in a manufacturing account for opening and closing work in progress.

7 A business manufactures office desks. The following information is available for the year ended 31 July 2018.

	$
Direct wages	82 600
Inventory raw materials at 1 August 2017	46 200
Inventory raw materials at 31 July 2018	49 700
Purchase of raw materials	415 300

Calculate the prime cost of manufacture for the year ended 31 July 2018.

8 A business manufactures furniture. The following information is available for the year ending 31 May 2018.

	$
Prime cost	225 000
Factory overheads	87 400
Opening work in progress	14 600
Closing work in progress	18 300

Calculate the cost of production for the year ended 31 May 2018.

Longer-Answer Questions

9 *Preparing a manufacturing account*

Choudhury & Co manufacture car seats. The following information is available for the year ended 30 April 2018.

	$
Direct wages	34 200
Factory insurance	8 600
Factory power	11 300
Factory rent	48 000
Factory supervisor's salary	12 100
Inventory: raw materials	
1 May 2017	26 700
30 April 2018	29 500
Machine depreciation	7 400
Machine maintenance	3 900
Purchase of raw materials	148 600

Prepare a manufacturing account for the year ended 30 April 2018.

10 *Preparing a manufacturing account with adjustments and work in progress*

Makumba & Co manufacture filing cabinets. The following information is available for the year ended 30 September 2018.

	$
Direct wages	65 360
Factory rent	36 600
Factory supervisor's salary	24 380
Insurance	12 600
Inventory: raw materials	
1 October 2017	21 100
30 September 2018	28 250
Inventory: work in progress	
1 October 2017	4 680
30 September 2018	5 230
Light, heat and power	14 500
Machine maintenance	6 670
Purchase of raw materials	163 840

Additional information at 30 September 2018:
- Factory supervisor's salary due but unpaid, $2120.
- Insurance should be shared: factory 75%, office 25%.
- Light, heat and power should be shared: factory 80%, office 20%.
- Factory machinery should be depreciated by $1280.
- Factory rent paid in advance, $2400.

Prepare a manufacturing account for the year ended 30 September 2018.

11 *Preparing a manufacturing account and an income statement*

Justin owns a manufacturing business. The following information is available for the year ended 30 June 2018.

	$
Administration salaries	12 120
Carriage outwards	2 550
Direct wages	83 420
Depreciation for the year: machinery	8 290
Depreciation for the year: delivery vehicles	6 760
Factory supervisor's salary	18 400
Indirect wages	42 090
Insurance	15 200
Inventory: finished goods	
1 July 2017	9 100
30 June 2018	11 400
Inventory: raw materials	
1 July 2017	18 700
30 June 2018	15 300
Inventory: work in progress	
1 July 2017	2 200
30 June 2018	3 950
Light, heat and power	12 250
Machine maintenance and repair	4 580
Property rental	24 000
Purchase of raw materials	188 650
Revenue	593 200
Salesmen's salaries	42 910

Additional information at 30 June 2018:

- Property rental should be shared: $\frac{4}{5}$ factory, $\frac{1}{5}$ office.
- Light, heat and power should be shared: $\frac{4}{5}$ factory, $\frac{1}{5}$ office.
- Insurance should be shared: $\frac{3}{4}$ factory, $\frac{1}{4}$ office.

Prepare:

a a manufacturing account for the year ended 30 June 2018

b an income statement for the year ended 30 June 2018.

> *GUIDANCE*
>
> *Remember that only factory costs can appear in a manufacturing account, and that all other non-factory costs appear in the income statement. A common error is to incorrectly record inventories. Raw materials and work in progress inventories appear in the manufacturing account, but finished goods inventories appear in the first part of the income statement.*

12 *Preparing the financial statements of a manufacturing business*

Davison & Co is a manufacturing business. The business's financial year ended on 31 May 2018 and the following trial balance was extracted.

	Dr	Cr
	$	$
Administration expenses	8 200	
Bank	6 580	
Capital		83 200
Direct wages	214 180	
Distribution expenses	39 350	
Drawings	81 210	
Factory general expenses	46 730	
Factory power	28 660	
Insurance	24 400	
Interest charges	3 940	
Inventory at 1 June 2017		
Finished goods	15 100	
Raw materials	12 700	
Work in progress	9 600	
Machinery at net book value	49 600	
Office equipment at net book value	14 200	
Office wages and salaries	22 050	
Property rental	81 200	
Purchases of raw materials	139 280	
Purchases of finished goods	12 310	
Revenue		829 140
Salesmen's salaries	52 370	
Trade payables		14 260
Trade receivables	64 940	
	926 600	926 600

Additional information at 31 May 2018:

- Inventories at 31 May 2018 were valued as follows: finished goods $14 600; raw materials $9800; work in progress $12 200.
- Office wages and salaries due at 31 May 2018 were $1250.
- Insurance paid in advance totalled $6400.
- Property rental should be shared: factory 80%; office 20%.
- Insurance should be shared: factory 75%; office 25%.
- Provide for depreciation of non-current assets as follows: machinery 20% per annum on net book value; office equipment 10% per annum on net book value.

Prepare:

a a manufacturing account for the year ended 31 May 2018

b an income statement for the year ended 31 May 2018

c a statement of financial position at 31 May 2018.

GUIDANCE

It is important to make an adjustment for the insurance paid in advance before calculating the amount to be charged to the manufacturing account and to the income statement. A common error is to show only a total for inventories in the statement of financial position – inventories should be shown as separate items.

> ## Introduction
> In this section there are questions to test your understanding of the reasons why some businesses do not make use of a full accounting system. There are questions requiring the use of techniques which are used to calculate a business's profit or loss where there are either very limited records (using a statement of affairs) or records which are just sufficient to make the preparation of financial statements possible, including the use of some accounting ratios to find missing figures.

Multiple Choice Questions

1 Susie has very limited accounting records. She is able to provide the following information about the year ended 31 August 2018.

	$
Capital, 1 September 2017	18 900
Capital, 31 August 2018	59 300
Drawings during the year ended 31 August 2018	14 800
Additional capital introduced on 1 May 2018	18 000

What is the business's profit for the year ended 31 August 2018?

a $7600   **b** $37 200   **c** $43 600   **d** $73 200

2 Leon is preparing statements of affairs for 1 January 2018 and 31 December 2018. He has included the following information in these statements:

	At 1 January 2018	At 31 December 2018
	$	$
Total assets	72 400	83 100
Total liabilities	17 300	19 500

Leon's drawings during the year ended 31 December 2018 totalled $17 500.

What is the business's profit or loss for the year ended 31 December 2018?

a loss $26 000   **b** loss $20 000   **c** profit $8500   **d** profit $26 000

3 Daniel is trying to calculate his business's revenue for the year ended 31 December 2018 from limited information. He is able to provide the following details.

	$
Trade receivables, 1 January 2018	3 400
Trade receivables, 31 December 2018	4 900
Amounts received from trade receivables during the year ended 31 December 2018	83 800

What is the business's revenue for the year ended 31 December 2018?

a $75 300   **b** $82 300   **c** $85 300   **d** $92 100

4 Tahir is preparing his business's income statement for the year ended 30 June 2018. He is able to provide the following information:

	$
Revenue for year ended 30 June 2018	80 000
Inventory 1 July 2017	18 000
Inventory 30 June 2018	15 000
Gross profit margin	40%

What was the total of the business's purchases for the year ended 30 June 2018?

a $29 000 **b** $35 000 **c** $45 000 **d** $51 000

Shorter-Answer Questions

5 State **two** reasons why the owner of a small business might not keep a full accounting system.

6 State the minimum information you would need to have in order to calculate the profit or loss for a business which has no accounting system.

7 Emilie owns a retail business selling the latest technology. However, she has kept only limited accounting records. The following information is available for the year ended 31 October 2018.

	$
Trade payables at 1 November 2017	7 280
Trade payables at 31 October 2018	6 930
Payments made to trade payables during the year ended 31 October 2018	74 880
Discounts received	1 490

In addition Emilie made cash purchases of $8470 during the year ended 31 October 2018. Calculate Emilie's total purchases for the year ended 31 October 2018.

8 The owner of a business has kept only basic accounting records. The following information is available about the year ended 31 December 2018.

	$
Revenue	160 000
Inventory, 1 January 2018	8 450
Inventory, 31 December 2018	7 550
Total expenses	44 300
Rate of inventory turnover	12

Set out a detailed calculation of the business's profit for the year ended 31 December 2018.

Longer-Answer Questions

9 *Preparing a statement of affairs and calculating a business's profit or loss*

owns a business. He has not kept detailed accounting records. On 1 September 2017 the business's capital was $82 400. At 31 August 2018 the following information was available.

	$
Cash at bank	8 240
Trade receivables	4 730
Trade payables	5 140
Inventory	6 770
Non-current assets	74 380
Bank loan	8 500

During the year ended 31 August 2018 Ombeya withdrew $17 350 from the business's bank account for private use. On 1 June 2018 he provided additional capital in the form of non-current assets valued at $11 400.

a Prepare a statement of affairs at 31 August 2018 to show the business's capital at this date.

b Calculate the profit or loss made by the business for the year ended 31 August 2018.

> *GUIDANCE*
>
> *An opening statement of affairs is a list of total assets less total liabilities, and the difference is the capital. A common mistake would be to alter the figure for non-current assets. The figure of $74 380 is at 31 August 2018, so it already includes the additional assets provided by the owner. You can set out the calculation of profit by showing a detailed capital section as part of the statement of affairs or as a separate calculation. When calculating profit or loss start by calculating the change in capital during the year and then add back drawings and deduct the additional capital. It is a common mistake to deduct drawings and add additional capital.*

10 *Calculating revenue and purchases*

Julie has not kept full accounting records for her business. At 31 October 2018 the following information is available.

	At 1 November 2017	At 31 October 2018
	$	$
Trade payables	17 340	21 200
Trade receivables	16 490	15 310

The business's cash book included the following details.

Cash Book (Bank columns) (extract)

	$		$
Receipts from trade receivables	105 430	Payments to trade payables	64 370
Cash takings banked	14 870	Cash purchases	1 480

Cash discounts of $480 were received from trade suppliers.

Calculate the business's total purchases and total revenue for the year ended 31 October 2018. Show detailed workings.

> **GUIDANCE**
>
> *Your workings could take the form of arithmetical calculations or ledger accounts as the question is not specific on this point. Whichever format you use, remember that anyone reading your work must be able to follow what you are doing, so clearly label each item. Remember also to include the cash purchases and cash sales in your final totals.*

11 *Preparing a complete income statement where there are incomplete records*

Anton owns a retail electrical business. He has chosen not to maintain a complete set of accounting records for his business. On 31 July 2018 he is able to present the following information concerning the year ended on that date.

	At 1 August 2017	At 31 July 2018
	$	$
Inventory	17 490	16 530
Rent prepaid	200	450
Trade payables	6 770	5 820
Trade receivables	3 790	4 480
Wages due	410	330

Cash Book (Bank columns) (extract)

	$		$
Receipts from trade receivables	82 490	Payments to trade payables	37 420
Cash takings banked	37 450	Cash purchases	3 370
		Rent	9 250
		Wages	23 440

Prepare:

a workings for information required for the preparation of an income statement for the year ended 31 July 2018

b an income statement for the year ended 31 July 2018.

> **GUIDANCE**
>
> *When calculating the correct amount to charge to the income statement for each expense, you may find it helpful to remember that information about adjustments which relate to the current year should be included; information relating to any other year should be excluded. For example, in the case of rent: the opening prepayment relates to rent for the current year so is included, the payment in the cash book is included, but the closing prepayment is excluded because it relates to next year.*

12 *Preparing a full set of financial statements from incomplete records with relatively straightforward information*

Greta owns a fashion store. She has not maintained a full set of accounts, but is able to supply the following information about the year ended 31 December 2018.

	At 1 January 2018	At 31 December 2018
	$	$
Cash at bank	3 320	2 170
Electricity charges due	120	-
Insurance prepaid	-	480
Inventory	11 160	15 430
Non-current assets at net book value	37 450	33 150
Trade payables	1 840	2 290
Trade receivables	2 990	2 320

Summarised Bank Account

	$		$
Opening balance	3 320	Payments to trade payables	43 850
Receipts from trade receivables	17 890	Drawings	22 490
Cash takings banked	84 350	General expenses	2 810
		Electricity	3 940
		Insurance	2 830
		Shop assistants' wages	27 470
		Closing balance c/d	2 170
	105 560		105 560
Balance b/d	2 170		

Prepare:

a an income statement for the year ended 31 December 2018

b a statement of affairs at 31 December 2018.

GUIDANCE

*It is important to provide detailed workings for all missing figures before you start to prepare the formal answer to task **a** and task **b**. The workings should include a calculation of the opening capital as this is needed for the final statement of affairs. A common error would be to overlook the fact that non-current assets have decreased in value during the year and a figure for depreciation should, therefore, be included in the income statement.*

---

13 *Preparing a full set of financial statements from incomplete records with more complex information including the use of an accounting ratio*

Arneford Wholesalers is owned by Whangi. He has not maintained a full set of accounting records for his business. The following information is available about the year ended 30 June 2018.

	At 1 July 2017	At 30 June 2018
	$	$
Bank overdraft	1 080	
Cash at bank		2 740
Inventory	11 160	?
Loan from bank	14 000	12 500
Non-current assets at net book value	85 900	93 200
Rent prepaid	1 480	930
Trade payables	11 990	10 200
Trade receivables	9 730	9 040
Wages due	1 220	910

Summarised Bank Account

	$		$
Receipts from trade receivables	189 860	Opening balance	1 080
Additional capital	9 000	Payments to trade payables	74 330
		Drawings	28 000
		Purchase of new non-current assets	12 000
		Loan from bank repayment	1 500
		Administration expenses	5 480
		Rent	22 400
		Wages	51 330
		Closing balance c/d	2 740
	198 860		198 860
Balance b/d	2 740		

Trade receivables were allowed cash discounts totalling $830 during the year ended 30 June 2018.

Whangi was unable to calculate the value of the business's closing inventory on 30 June 2018. However, he is able to inform you that the business always achieves a gross margin of 60%.

Prepare:

a an income statement for the year ended 30 June 2018

b a statement of affairs at 30 June 2018.

GUIDANCE

This question has many features to fully test the skills required to prepare financial statements from incomplete records. As always ensure that detailed workings are provided. It is important to notice some particular elements in the question which could easily be overlooked, for example: the fact that the opening bank balance is overdrawn when calculating the opening capital; the introduction of additional capital during the year; the purchase of additional non-current assets which will affect the calculation of the year's depreciation charge, etc. It would be easy to forget to include the discounts allowed in the income statement, and to make a mistake concerning the repayment of the bank loan by including this amount in the income statement.

Introduction

In this section you will have the opportunity to test your knowledge and skills of accounting ratios and also of how to interpret these ratios.

You will recall that information in financial statements is used by interested parties to assess the performance of a business. It enables the users to make decisions and plan for the future. In order to do this, the figures from financial statements are converted into accounting ratios. These ratios are then used for comparison and assessment. The accounting ratios based on the income statements measure profitability. The accounting ratios based on the statement of financial position measure liquidity and the business's financial position. The ratios are analysed and interpreted to enable the users to assess, make decisions and plan. However, there are limitations in the use of these ratios in isolation from other key facts about a business.

Multiple Choice Questions

1 What is the formula for the profit margin?

a Gross profit for the year divided by revenue

b Profit for the year divided by capital

c Profit for the year divided by cost of sales

d Profit for the year divided by revenue

2 The following information relates to a business:

	$
Opening inventory	15 000
Purchases	60 000
Revenue	85 000
Closing inventory	19 000

What is the annual rate of inventory turnover?

a 2.9 times   **b** 3.3 times   **c** 3.5 times   **d** 5 times

3 Which of the following is **not** required when calculating the current ratio?

a Motor vehicles   **b** Other payables   **c** Trade payables   **d** Trade receivables

4 The percentage gross margin for a business for two years was:

Year 1   30%
Year 2   35%

Which of the following would be one possible reason for the change?

a Average inventory was lower

b Cost price per unit had increased

c Expenses had decreased

d Selling price per unit had increased

Shorter-Answer Questions

5 A summary of B Collins's income statement for the year ended 31 December 2018 was:

Income Statement for the year ended 31 December 2018

	$	$
Revenue		95 000
Opening inventory	18 000	
Add Purchases	40 000	
	58 000	
Less Closing inventory	(12 000)	
Cost of sales		(46 000)
Gross profit		49 000
Less expenses		(30 000)
Profit for the year		19 000

a Calculate to **two** decimal places the following ratios. Show the formula used. Show workings.

   i Percentage gross margin

   ii Percentage profit margin

   iii Rate of inventory turnover

b Explain the meaning of the rate of inventory turnover ratio.

6 Helen's statement of financial position at 31 December 2018 is given below:

	$	$
Non-current assets		120 000
Current assets		
Inventory	15 000	
Trade receivables	30 000	
Other receivables	2 000	47 000
		167 000
Capital		
Balance (31 December 2018)		112 000
Non-current liabilities		
Bank loan		24 000
Current liabilities		
Trade payables	26 000	
Bank	5 000	31 000
		167 000

Other information – profit for the year

- Revenue $192 000
- Purchases $154 000
- Profit $18 000

a Calculate to **two** decimal places the following ratios:

   i Current ratio

   ii Liquid (acid test) ratio

iii Trade receivables turnover
iv Trade payables payment period
v Return on capital employed

b Comment on the result of the return on capital employed.

Longer-Answer Questions

7 *Calculate profitability and liquidity ratios*

The financial statements of T Harrison are given below:

Income Statement for the year ended 31 March 2018

	$	$
Revenue		115 000
Opening inventory	16 000	
Add Purchases	78 000	
	94 000	
Less Closing inventory	(18 000)	
Cost of sales		(76 000)
Gross profit		39 000
Less Expenses		(25 000)
Profit for the year		14 000

Statement of Financial Position at 31 March 2018

	$	$
Non-current assets		48 500
Current assets		
Inventory	6 000	
Trade receivables	15 500	
Bank	7 500	29 000
		77 500
Capital		
Opening balance		44 200
Add Profit for the year		14 000
		58 200
Less Drawings		(8 000)
		50 200
Non-current liabilities		
Bank loan		9 000
Current liabilities		
Trade payables	16 300	
Other payables	2 000	18 300
		77 500

Prepare to **one** decimal place the following ratios:

a Percentage gross margin

b Percentage profit margin

c Rate of inventory turnover

d Return on capital employed

e Current ratio

f Liquid (acid test) ratio

g Trade receivables turnover

h Trade payables payment period

> **GUIDANCE**
>
> *When calculating a ratio always show the formula and the workings (i.e. the figures you have extracted from the information in the question). Ensure that the answer is given to one decimal place as specifically requested in this question. Always give the answer a descriptor, e.g. % or times, etc.*

8 *Calculate and analyse profitability ratios of two businesses*

The following are summary income statements for two businesses.

Income Statement for the year ended 31 December 2018

		Larry		Bob
		$000		$000
Revenue		400		520
Opening inventory	29		44	
Add Purchases	323		375	
	352		419	
Less Closing inventory	(35)	(317)	(42)	(377)
Gross profit		83		143
Less Expenses		(52)		(70)
Profit for the year		31		73

a Calculate to **two** decimal places the following ratios for each business:

i Percentage gross margin

ii Percentage profit margin

iii Rate of inventory turnover

b State which business is the most profitable, and give **two** reasons for your answer.

> **GUIDANCE**
>
> *Make sure that you always name clearly the business you are describing. Do not explain the meaning of the ratio unless specifically asked to do so. When answering part **b** it is a good idea to begin each reason as a new paragraph, so that both reasons are clearly separate.*

9 *Analyse the liquidity ratios of two years*

The following ratios were calculated for Jessica's business for two years.

	For the year ended 31 December	
	2017	**2018**
Current ratio	2:1	2.5:1
Liquid (acid test) ratio	0.4:1	0.6:1
Trade receivables turnover	36 days	35 days
Trade payables payment period	30 days	31 days

a Explain the meaning of:

   i the current ratio

   ii the liquid (acid test) ratio.

b Comment on the change in **each** ratio, and give **one** reason for the change.

c Comment on the overall liquidity position of Jessica's business. Give reasons for your answer.

> *GUIDANCE*
>
> *Make a judgement for each ratio, e.g. improved or deteriorated. It is a common error merely to state that a ratio is now higher or lower as this does not clarify whether it is a good thing or a bad thing for the business.*

Introduction

In this section there are questions to test your understanding of the accounting principles and concepts that govern the preparation of accounting records together with the accounting policies that are adopted by businesses when producing financial statements.

Multiple Choice Questions

1 Chad purchased a new motor vehicle as a present for his son. He paid $4000 for the vehicle, but estimated that it was worth $4500. Chad recorded the purchase in the drawings account.

This is an example of the application of which one of the following principles?

a Accruals

b Business entity

c Money measurement

d Prudence

2 Imran accounts for depreciation on his plant and machinery at 15% per annum using the reducing balance method.

This is an example of the application of which one of the following principles?

a Accruals

b Going concern

c Prudence

d Realisation

3 Vikram owns a shop selling computer equipment. On the last day of his financial year, his cash sales for the day amounted to $2100. On the same day he received an order from a regular credit customer for $3500. His total sales for the day were entered in his records as $2100.

This is an example of the application of which one of the following principles?

a Accruals

b Consistency

c Prudence

d Realisation

4 Sara sold goods on credit four months ago to a new customer for $1200. Sara has still not received the money owing and makes a provision for doubtful debts for the full amount outstanding in her financial statements.

This is an example of the application of which one of the following principles?

a Prudence

b Consistency

c Money measurement

d Realisation

5 Businesses should value their inventory at the lower of cost or net realisable value.

This is an example of the application of which one of the following principles?

a Accruals

b Consistency

c Money measurement

d Prudence

6 Jake is preparing his accounts for the year ended 30 June 2018. On 1 April 2018 he paid $5000 rent for the 6 months ending 30 September 2018. He is to provide for a prepayment of one half of this payment in his financial statements.

This is an example of the application of which one of the following principles?

a Accruals

b Consistency

c Duality

d Prudence

7 Tom's inventory included one item that cost $815 and had a selling price of $960. The item needed repair at a cost of $50. After repair, the item could be sold for $850.

At what value should the item be recorded in Tom's inventory?

a $765

b $800

c $815

d $850

Shorter-Answer Questions

8 Explain briefly what is meant by the money measurement principle.

9 Explain briefly what is meant by the principle of duality.

10 Explain briefly what is meant by the consistency principle. Give an example to illustrate your answer.

11 Steven owns a chain of five electrical shops. He purchased a new printer for $180 that he expects will have a useful life of three years.

Advise Steven how he should record this transaction in his financial statements. State the accounting principle that this is based upon.

12 Bharti owns a shop selling televisions. She is valuing the shop's inventory at her year-end and finds that one of the televisions has been damaged. The television cost $430 and the usual selling price is $550. Bharti believes that it will cost $80 to repair and after repair, she will be able to sell the television at a reduced price of $520.

a Calculate the value that Bharti should enter in her inventory at the year-end.

b State the accounting principle that applies.

13 International accounting standards are designed to protect those who use accounting statements and stop them being misled. Explain the following four headings:

- comparability
- relevance
- reliability
- understandability

Longer-Answer Question

14 *Applying Accounting Principles and Concepts*

Janine has been running a wholesale business for the past three years. Her financial year ended on 31 March 2018 and she is unsure how to deal with some transactions at that date.

i During the year she paid $2000 to take her family on holiday. She has charged the amount to general expenses in her accounting records.

ii Janine has counted all of her inventory at 31 March 2018 and has found that some items are damaged. The items cost $340 and had a selling price of $450. Janine believes that it will cost $60 to have the items repaired and that she will then be able to sell them for $425.

iii Janine's business has been very successful over the three years with a large number of regular customers. The customers are very enthusiastic about the way Janine and her staff run the business and she views this as a real asset to her business. In preparing her accounts, she wonders what value she should place on this asset.

iv For the first two years of her business, Janine depreciated her non-current assets using the straight line method. She has been advised that it may be better to change to the reducing balance method and she is unsure whether she should do this.

v On 31 March 2018, Janine sent goods to the value of $2300 to a regular customer. She has not received any cash from the customer because she has not had time to prepare the invoice yet. As the customer has accepted the goods, she has entered the $2300 sale in her records on 31 March 2018.

Advise Janine how to deal with each of the above points. State the accounting principle that you are using.

GUIDANCE

In each case it is important to clearly state the name of the accounting principle you think applies to the situation. However, do not just give the name of the principle; give a brief explanation of the principle. Then state concisely how each situation should be dealt with. When you have finished, read through your answer and ask yourself, 'Would Janine now understand the correct treatment of each point?'

Here are some ideas to help you to improve your performance.

During Your Course of Study

Your Course File

With the help of your teacher, you should aim to build up a file of questions and answers which you can easily access when you start to revise for the examination. It is important that you have a wide range of questions and answers covering all the key elements in the specification. The answers might be your own work which include indications of any errors and maybe corrections, but might also include model answers provided by your teacher or taken from mark schemes.

Learning from your Mistakes

When you check your work, as well as feeling pleased about all the things you managed to get right, do make a point of focusing on what went wrong. Use a model answer to work out the nature of your mistake and spend some time getting to understand what the correct answer should have been. You may, of course, need the help of a teacher for this. It is a very good idea to 'repair' your answer. This means pencilling in a correction (as long as you understand how this was achieved). There is much evidence from international research that this idea of focusing on mistakes and repairing answers if carried out systematically can have a dramatic effect on performance with students achieving higher grades than would otherwise have been the case. By the way, this idea of 'repairing' works really well for prose answers, too. Pencil in any points you did not include in your answer and strike out any points which were not relevant.

Before the Examination

Revision

This is where that course file will be of great value, particularly if it is comprehensive and well organised. The key to successful revision is to actually answer (or reanswer) questions, not just to look through answers prepared before. So try reworking questions on topics you feel less confident about. Make sure you have the model answer or at least a corrected answer available, so that when you get stuck you can check up on the right answer. Avoid using model answers until you really have to, of course. Try doing some questions under strict time conditions, too, and do answer the whole question, don't avoid the prose response sections, for example. As part of your revision check through the course specification to make sure you have covered everything.

Using past Examination Papers

Practising on past examination papers will make a lot of difference to your confidence and, of course, your awareness of what to expect in the examination room. Use the mark schemes not only to check and 'repair' your work, but also to help you gain an understanding of what the examiners are looking for. In the case of prose answers, for example, you will gain an appreciation of the length of answer required. Many exam candidates' prose answers are too brief and therefore score badly, or are too lengthy, which means candidates have wasted valuable time.

Your Examination Answers

Here are some ideas which should help you improve the quality of your answers.

Time Allocation

Try to divide up the time available for the questions in proportion to the marks available.

Try to avoid over-running on any one question as it simply means you will have to rush on another. Remember that you usually earn marks more quickly at the beginning of an answer and rather more slowly at the end.

Reading the Question

Do check that you have read the actual question requirements carefully. It is so easy to waste time by providing information which is not required, or missing out some vital element expected by the examiner. Here are some examples:

Do provide an account if the question asks for it. It is surprising to learn that some candidates think that a calculation will suffice when an account is required. In the case of prose questions, do not give a one-word answer if the question asks for an explanation. An explanation requires at least a sentence or two, i.e. some development, so that you demonstrate a good understanding of the subject matter of the question.

Do go through the question data over and over again. For example, as you know some questions contain a lot of information, it would be all too easy to overlook an item in a trial balance or an adjustment required by details in one of the notes following a trial balance.

Workings

Workings are a crucial element in so many answers, so it is vital that you do not leave the examiner to guess how you obtained a particular figure. Take the trouble to make your workings easy to follow. It is good practice to avoid providing a string of figures – a more carefully labelled list of figures is much more helpful. Students who have got used to providing detailed workings throughout the course are far less likely to forget about this when it comes to the stresses of the actual exam. In many cases there are many marks allocated to workings, which can be lost if the workings are omitted and the answer to the calculation is incorrect.

Focus on Matters of Detail

The following points are considered good practice.

Preparing and Balancing an Account

It is best practice to state the year on each side of the account, to date each entry. It is acceptable to abbreviate the month to just three letters (e.g. Mar, Aug) in the confined space provided for the date.

Always bring down any balance on an account. The balance brought down should be dated for the beginning of the next period. Many students are often not very well skilled in the technique of balancing accounts.

Presentation and Headings

As you know there are very strict rules about the presentation of financial statements which you must follow. These rules have been developed to ensure that users are given clear and precise information. If available, give the name of the business first. Avoid using abbreviations in headings. Many students spoil otherwise good answers by using y/e for year ending or reducing the date to a few letters such as Dec for December, for example. Do not use GP, CoS, etc. for labels within an income statement; always write labels in full.

Under exam pressure it is quite likely that you will be rushed at times and that you will want to make changes to your answers. Try to ensure that all of your work is legible, however rushed you are. When you need to change an answer, try to make sure that your final answer is legible. A common problem is that some students write a new figure over an existing figure, and it becomes very difficult or almost impossible to determine exactly what was intended.

Ratios

When calculating ratios make sure your answer is given showing the number of decimal places required. If you need to round a decimal, apply the rule of 5 and above is rounded up; below 5 is rounded down. If you are required to calculate a ratio to two decimal places, but the answer is actually a whole number, then, for example, show an answer of 25% as 25.00%.

You are often required to make some judgement about a business's performance when using ratios. It is a common mistake to describe what has happened rather than to assess how well a business is doing. For example an answer such as 'the ratio has increased' does not convey whether this is a good or bad thing for the business. It is important to say 'the ratio has improved' or 'the ratio has weakened' as the case may be.

Prose Answers

Aim to be as precise in writing your prose answers as you are with numerical work. It is good practice to include the name of the business you are writing about and to show a good level of understanding by using appropriate accounting terminology. It is easy to spoil an answer by being vague: profit (when you mean gross profit); assets (when you mean current assets); profit will be affected (when you mean profit will be increased).

Sometimes you will be asked to explain a difference between two accounting terms. It is important to refer to both elements in your answer. For example, if you are asked to explain the difference between trade and cash discount, a weak answer would be 'trade discount is given for bulk buying; cash discount is not'. Much better to say 'trade discount is given for bulk buying; cash discount is given for prompt payment'.

Introduction

In this final section you will have the opportunity to test yourself on a wide range of topics and on a variety of question styles, including multiple choice, questions requiring computational answers and questions requiring a prose response.

There are two sets of practice questions. You may like to try a set of questions as a test and put into practice some of the advice and suggestions given in Section 13 (Improving your performance).

Further Practice Questions Set 1

1 A Hall buys $450 of goods on credit less 33⅓ % trade discount and 2½% cash discount.

What amount will he pay if he settles his account within the agreed time?

a $292.50

b $292.65

c $300.15

d £307.50

2 Jean White was charged bank interest.

Which source document should be used to record this transaction?

a Bank statement

b Cash receipt

c Cheque counterfoil

d Invoice

3 Cash of $300 is withdrawn from the bank for business use.

What is the double entry to record this transaction?

a Dr – Bank $300   Cr – Cash $300

b Dr – Cash $300   Cr – Bank $300

c Dr – Drawings $300   Cr – Bank $300

d Dr – Drawings $300   Cr – Cash $300

4 The following information is available for a business:

	$
Revenue	76 000
Cost of sales	35 500
Expenses	28 800
Capital employed	92 000

What is the return on capital employed?

a 12.7%

b 15.4%

c 44.0%

d 53.3%

5 On 1 May 2017 the Park Social Club had subscriptions in arrears of $56 and subscriptions in advance of $114. During the year subscriptions were received of $5420. At 30 April 2018 there were subscriptions in arrears of $92.

What was the subscription income for the year?

a $5270

b $5386

c $5454

d $5570

6 Sean Roberts is a customer of Paul May. On 1 April 2018 he owed him $750. The following transactions took place in April:

Apr   3   Sold goods to Sean Roberts $570, less 30% trade discount

        7   Sean paid by cheque the amount owing on 1 April in full settlement, less 2% cash discount

      11   Sold goods to Sean Roberts $180, less 20% trade discount

      23   Sean Roberts returned goods bought on 3 April $120

Prepare Sean Roberts's account as it would appear in Paul May's ledger for the month of April 2018.

7 The table below contains transactions carried out in the month of February 2018.

	Source document	Book of prime entry	Effect on profit
a Sold goods on credit $620, less 25% trade discount			
b Received a cheque in full settlement of $250 owed, less 2% cash discount			
c Bought equipment on credit $840			
d Paid postage in cash $46			

Complete the table for each transaction.

8 On 30 April 2018 Katy produced a draft profit for the year of $36 400.

The following errors were subsequently discovered:

i   the purchases journal was overstated by $300

ii   wages $180 were correctly entered in the cash book, but were credited to the wages account

iii   a sales invoice to Kim $256 had not been entered in the books

iv   a credit note from a supplier C Brown for $98 had been entered in the purchases returns journal as $89.

a Prepare general journal entries, with suitable narratives, to correct the errors i–iv.

b Prepare a statement of corrected profit, after the correction of errors i–iv.

9 On 1 May 2018 Peter Phillips is owed $5210 by his customer Julia Jones. Julia Jones is declared bankrupt and agreed to pay 20 cents for each dollar owed.

On 30 May 2018 she sent a cheque to Peter in settlement. The balance on her account was written off as an irrecoverable debt.

a Prepare the general journal entry, with a suitable narrative, to write off Julia's account.

b Advise Peter why he should create a provision for doubtful debts.

10 The following information relates to a business at 30 April 2018.

	$
Capital	66 000
Revenue	55 000
Expenses	18 000
Inventory	16 000
Trade payables	7 000
Trade receivables	12 400
Bank overdraft	5 600

The business's percentage profit to revenue ratio is 10%.

Calculate the:

a cost of sales

b gross margin ratio

c current ratio

d liquid (acid test) ratio.

11 Ahmed provided the following information for the year ended 31 January 2018:

	$
Opening inventory	18 320
Closing inventory	21 150
Cost of sales	90 000
Expenses	12 900
Capital employed	120 000
Mark-up	25%

a For the year ended 31 January 2018, calculate

i revenue

ii gross profit

iii profit for the year.

b Calculate the following ratios to **one** decimal place.

i Gross margin

ii Profit margin

iii Rate of inventory turnover

iv Return on capital employed

c Ahmed's comparative ratios for the year ended 31 January 2017 were:

i gross margin 26.4%

ii profit margin 12.3%

iii rate of inventory turnover 4.8 times

iv return on capital employed 10.4%

Give **two** comments on the performance of Ahmed's business over the two years.

d Suggest **two** actions Ahmed could take to improve the return on capital employed.

12 The receipts and payments account of the Crofts Sports Club for the year ended 30 June 2018 was as follows:

	$		$
Balance b/d	1 400	Match expenses	5 436
Subscriptions	12 140	General expenses	4 132
Match fees	7 360	Purchases of refreshments	3 250
Sales of refreshments	6 436	Equipment	7 820
		Wages	2 320
		Balance c/d	4 378
	27 336		27 336

Additional information:

Balances at	1 July 2017	30 June 2018
Equipment at valuation	6 000	12 200
Subscriptions in arrears	180	220
Subscriptions in advance	320	260
Inventory of refreshments	530	590
Trade payables (refreshments)	720	660

Of the wages $800 relates to refreshments.

a For the year ended 30 June 2018, prepare the:
  i subscriptions account
  ii refreshments account.

b Calculate the depreciation on equipment for the year.

c Name the type of depreciation used to calculate the depreciation on equipment.

13 Lynn's trial balance at 30 June 2018 did not agree, and a suspense account was opened.
The following errors were subsequently discovered:
  i The total of the purchases returns journal had been undercast by $74
  ii A payment for wages $670 had been correctly entered in the cash book, but was recorded in the wages account as $760
  iii A credit sale $350 to J Brown had been entered in W Brown's account
  iv Rent paid $175 had been recorded in the rent account twice
  v The discount received was undercast by $17

a Prepare the entries in the general journal to correct the errors i – v.

b Prepare a suspense account at 30 June 2018 and show the original difference in the trial balance.

14 David Scott has the following assets and liabilities at 1 July 2018:

	$
Non-current assets	24 000
Trade receivables	12 230
Trade payables	8 670
Inventory	5 140
Insurance prepaid	380
General expenses accrued	140
Bank overdraft	1 170
Bank loan	2 500
Capital	?

Prepare an opening general journal entry, with a suitable narrative, to show the opening capital at 1 July 2018.

Further Practice Questions Set 2

1 A trader's year-end is 30 June 2018. During the year he had paid $6200 for heating and lighting. At 1 July 2017, the amount owing was $520. The charge to the trader's income statement was $6500.

What was the balance brought down on the heating and lighting account at 30 June 2018?

a $220 credit

b $820 credit

c $220 debit

d $820 debit

2 The following figures have been extracted from the manufacturing account of a business.

Prime cost	$85 000
Factory overheads	$15 000
Opening work in progress	$6 000
Closing work in progress.	$4 000

What is the production cost of finished goods?

a $96 000

b $98 000

c $102 000

d $110 000

3 The Raleigh Fishing Club has 200 members. Each member pays an annual subscription of $80. At 1 September 2017, $400 had been paid in advance by members and $640 was owing. At 31 August 2018, $200 had been paid in advance and $320 was owing. $16 000 was included as subscriptions in the income and expenditure account.

What is the total amount of subscriptions received in the year ended 31 August 2018?

a $15 640

b $16 000

c $16 120

d $16 360

4 Which one of the following expenses should appear on the credit side of a trial balance?

   a Carriage inwards

   b Carriage outwards

   c Returns inwards

   d Returns outwards

5 Which one of the following errors will affect the agreement of the trial balance totals?

   a A payment for motor expenses has been posted to the motor vehicles account

   b A payment for rent has been omitted from the accounting records

   c A payment for repairs has been debited to the bank account and credited to the repairs account

   d The total of the sales journal has been undercast

6 Alan owns a wholesale business. He extracted the following trial balance at his year end, 30 June 2018.

	Dr $	Cr $
Bank loan (repayable 2023)		24 000
Bank		5 190
Capital at 1 July 2017		73 245
Cash in hand	400	
Discount received		1 290
Drawings	42 940	
Equipment – cost	58 900	
Equipment – provision for depreciation at 1 July 2017		22 100
General expenses	28 840	
Inventory at 1 July 2017	62 000	
Motor vehicles - cost	38 000	
Motor vehicles – provision for depreciation at 1 July 2017		13 600
Provision for doubtful debts		285
Purchases	166 800	
Rent and rates	31 100	
Sales returns	2 510	
Purchases returns		1 020
Revenue		323 400
Trade payables		18 180
Trade receivables	38 400	
Wages and salaries	12 420	
	482 310	482 310

Additional information:

i Inventory at 30 June 2018 was valued at $51 500.

ii General expenses of $1680 was still owing at 30 June 2018.

iii Rent and rates prepaid at 30 June 2018 amounted to $2400.

iv The bank loan was received on 1 March 2018. Interest is to be charged at 8% per annum.

v During the year, Alan took goods for his own use with a cost price of $1900. No entry has been made in the accounting records for this.

vi Depreciation on motor vehicles is to be charged at 20% per annum using the reducing balance method. Depreciation on equipment is to be charged at 10% per annum using the straight line method.

vii The provision for doubtful debts is to be maintained at 1% of trade receivables.

a Prepare the income statement of Alan for the year ended 30 June 2018.

b Prepare the statement of financial position of Alan at 30 June 2018.

c Alan makes a provision for doubtful debts in his financial statements. Which accounting principle is this an example of?

d State three reasons why a provision for depreciation is made on non-current assets.

7 Arthur and Ben are in partnership sharing profits and losses in the ration 3:2. In addition, the partnership agreement provides for the following:

- Partners are entitled to interest on capital of 5% per annum.
- Interest on drawings is provided at 6% per annum.
- Ben is entitled to a salary of $8000 per annum.

The following information is available for the year ended 31 August 2018.

- The balances on the partners' capital accounts at 1 September 2017 were: Arthur $60 000, Ben $30 000.
- The balances on the partners' current accounts at 1 September 2017 were: Arthur $26 330 Credit, Ben $6180 Debit.
- The profit of the partnership before appropriation was $44 212.
- Partners' drawings for the year were: Arthur $27 500, Ben $22 300.
- Ben introduced an additional $10 000 capital on 2 September 2017.

a Prepare the appropriation account for the partnership for the year ended 31 August 2018.

b Prepare the partners' capital accounts at 31 August 2018.

c Prepare the partners' current accounts at 31 August 2018.

d Explain the significance of the opening debit balance on Ben's current account.

8 Sagbo & Co is a manufacturing business. The following information is available for the year ended 30 April 2018.

	$
Carriage inwards	1 840
Direct wages	43 750
Factory supervisor's salary	28 200
Insurance	14 800
Inventory: raw materials	
1 May 2017	28 420
30 April 2018	25 600
Inventory: work in progress	
1 May 2017	12 360
30 April 2018	9 370
Light, heat and power	12 600
Machine maintenance	5 090
Purchase of raw materials	214 110
Rent and rates	45 620

Additional information at 30 September 2018:

- Factory supervisor's salary due but unpaid, $1430.
- Rent and rates paid in advance $3620.
- Insurance should be shared: factory 75%, office 25%.
- Light, heat and power should be shared: factory 80%, office 20%.
- Rent and rates should be shared: factory 4/5, office 1/5.
- Factory machinery should be depreciated by $2600.

a Prepare a manufacturing account for the year ended 30 September 2018.

b Explain the difference between direct costs and indirect costs.

c Explain how the accruals (matching) principle has affected the preparation of the manufacturing account.

9 The Lakeside Fishing Club charges its members an annual subscription of $80 each.

At 1 January 2018, twelve members had yet to pay their subscriptions for the year. During the year ended 31 December 2018, a total of $6800 was received from members for annual subscriptions. This figure included $560 received in advance from members for subscriptions 2019, but six members had failed to pay their subscriptions for 2018.

a Prepare a subscriptions account for 2018.

b Explain what is meant by the accumulated fund of a club or society and how this arises.

10 The following information has been extracted from the financial statements of L Ltd for the year ended 31 August 2018.

	$000
Bank (credit balance)	23
Capital employed	180
Inventory at 1 September 2017	52
Inventory at 31 August 2018	60
Operating expenses	136
Other payables	9
Other receivables	3
Purchases	165
Revenue	340
Trade payables	32
Trade receivables	55

All sales and purchases were on credit.

a Calculate the gross profit for the year for L Ltd.
b Calculate the profit for the year for L Ltd.
c Calculate the following ratios to **one** decimal place. State the formula used.
   i Gross margin
   ii Profit margin
   iii Current ratio
   iv Liquid (acid test) ratio
   v Trade receivables turnover
   vi Trade payables turnover
   vii Return on capital employed

The directors of L Ltd understand that businesses in a similar line to themselves are returning a gross profit percentage of around 60%. Advise the directors of **two** ways in which L Ltd could improve its gross profit percentage.

SECTION 1 BASIC DOUBLE-ENTRY RECORDS

Multiple Choice Questions

1 d   **2** b   **3** c   **4** a

Shorter-Answer Questions

5 To inform the owner about: how profitable the business is, whether the business has sufficient cash resources to pay its commitments on time, if the business is making the best use of its resources.

6 a Debit Bank, Credit Cash
  b Debit Drawings, Credit Cash
  c Debit Trade receivables, Credit Sales
  d Debit Cash, Credit Trade receivables
  e Debit Cash, Credit Office equipment
  f Debit Bank, Credit Bank loan
  g Debit Purchases, Credit Trade payables

7 To check the arithmetical accuracy of the double entry records.

8 a Credit   **f** Debit
  b Debit   **g** Credit
  c Debit   **h** Credit
  d Debit   **i** Debit
  e Credit   **j** Debit

Longer-Answer Questions

9 a Capital 15 040 (Assets 4580 plus 18 460 less Liability 8000)

  b and **c**

Bank Debit: May 1 Balance 4580, May 17 Sales 2930; May 23 Trade receivables 5800; May 25 Office equipment and furniture 250

Credit: May 7 Drawings 750, May 8 Office equipment and furniture 1840, May 11 Rent 840, May 13 Trade payables 14 300, May 20 Bank loan 1000

Capital Credit: May 1 Balance 15 040

Drawings Debit: May 7 Bank 750

Loan from bank Debit: May 20 Bank 1000,

Credit: May 1 Balance 8000

Purchases Debit: May 2 Trade payables 17 400

Rent Debit: May 11 Bank 840

Sales Credit: May 6 Trade receivables 8300, May 17 Bank 2930

Trade payables Debit: May 13 Bank 14 300,

Credit: May 2 Purchases 17 400

Trade receivables Debit: May 6 Sales 8300,
Credit: May 23 Bank 5800

10 Aug 1 Purchased goods and paid by cheque 3700

Aug 2 Sold goods on credit 4140

Aug 3 Borrowed 11 000 from bank; the funds were transferred to business's bank account

Aug 4 Purchases goods on credit 6200

Aug 5 Cash sales 1900

Aug 6 Transferred cash 1700 to business bank account

Aug 7 Owner withdrew cash 150 for private use

Aug 8 Paid trade payables 4800 by cheque

Aug 9 Received a cheque from trade receivables 4140

Aug 10 Withdrew cash 500 from business bank account

Aug 11 Paid loan interest 100; funds were withdrawn from business's bank account

11 *Debit items*: administration expenses 6780, cash in hand 130, drawings 13 540, non-current assets 75 400, purchases 62 390, trade receivables 7380, wages and salaries 18 240

Credit items: bank overdraft 1910, capital 56 000, loan from bank 10 000, sales 110 480, trade payables 5470

Trial balance totals: 183 860

12 a and **b**

Bank Debit: Aug 1 Balance 3740, Aug 4 Trade receivables 1070, Aug 10 Cash 600, Aug 18 Capital 3500

Credit: Aug 6 Loan interest 80, Aug 14 Trade payables 2800, Aug 22 Bank loan 1400, Aug 27 Motor vehicle 7200, Aug 28 Rent 610

Bank loan Debit: Aug 22 Bank 1400,

Credit: Aug 1 Balance 6000

Capital Credit: Aug 1 Balance 44 380, Aug 18 Bank 3500

Cash Debit: Aug 1 Balance 390, Aug 9 Sales 1720,

Credit: Aug 2 Drawings 230, Aug 10 Bank 600, Aug 24 General expenses 330, Aug 30 Wages 840

Drawings Debit: Aug 1 Balance 18 330, Aug 2 Cash 230

General expenses Debit: Aug 1 Balance 2200, Aug 24 Cash 330

Loan interest Debit: Aug 1 Balance 480, Aug 6 Bank 80

Motor vehicles Debit: Aug 1 Balance 32 400, Aug 27 Bank 7200

Purchases Debit: Aug 1 Balance 39 010, Aug 3 Trade payables 3850

Rent Debit: Aug 1 Balance 5570, Aug 28 Bank 610

Sales Credit: Aug 1 Balance 59 880, Aug 9 Cash 1720, Aug 12 Trade receivables 6340

Trade payables Debit: Aug 14 Bank 2800,

Credit: Aug 1 Balance 3390, Aug 3 Purchases 3850

Trade receivables Debit: Aug 1 Balance 2680, Aug 12 Sales 6340,

Credit: Aug 4 Bank 1070

Wages Debit: Aug 1 Balance 8850, Aug 30 Cash 840

c *Trial balance*

Debit items: Cash 110, Drawings 18 560, General expenses 2530, Loan interest 560, Motor vehicles 39 600, Purchases 42 860, Rent 6180, Trade receivables 7950, Wages 9690

Credit items: Bank overdraft 3180, Bank loan 4600, Capital 47 880, Sales 67 940, Trade payables 4440

Trial balance totals: 128 040

SECTION 2 DEVELOPING THE DOUBLE-ENTRY SYSTEM

Multiple Choice Questions

1 b   **2** b   **3** c   **4** c   **5** a   **6** b   **7** a   **8** b

Shorter-Answer Questions

9 a *Purchases Journal* Blacks Ltd 1056, T Harvey 1600, M Brown 799, J Williams 504, T Harvey 1000, Total 4959

   Purchases Returns Journal T Harvey 180, J Williams 72, Total 252

   b *Purchases Ledger* Dr: T Harvey 180, J Williams 72,

   Cr: Blacks Ltd 1056, T Harvey 1600, 1000, M Brown 799, J Williams 504

   c *Nominal Ledger* Dr: Purchases 4959,

   Cr: Purchases returns 252

10 a *Sales Ledger* Dr: P Watson 734 845, L Johnson 2 370 940, A Hunter 1 432 433,

   Cr: P Watson 135, L Johnson 250, A Hunter 74

   b *Nominal Ledger* Dr: Sales returns 459,

   Dr: Sales 6754

Longer-Answer Questions

11 a Dr: 200.00

   Cr: postage 18.10, stationery 40.20, office expenses 23.40, purchases ledger 67.30

   b *Debit* – total 200.00, balance b/d 51.00, bank 149.00

   Credit – total payments 149.00, balance c/d 51.00, total 200.00

12 Aug 1 Dr: Fixtures and fittings 18 000, motor vehicles 5000, inventory 7200, total 30 200

   Cr: Trade payables 6300, bank 2400, capital 21 500, total 30 200

   Assets and liabilities at this date

   3 Dr: Motor vehicles 2500, Cr: L Walker 2500

   Motor vehicles bought on credit, invoice no 69

   8 Dr: Drawings 125, Cr: Purchases 125

   Goods taken for private use

   15 Dr: J Peters 390, Cr: T Porter 390

   Sales to J Peters entered in T Porter's account

   20 Dr: P Webb 250, Cr: Equipment 250

   Equipment sold on credit to P Webb, invoice no 1235

   31 Dr: Income statement 25 000, Cr: Purchases 25 000

   Purchases transferred to the income statement

   31 Dr: Discount received 170, Cr: Income statement 170

   Discount received transferred to the income statement

13 a Cash book

b Purchases journal

c General journal

d Cash book

e Sales returns journal

f General journal

g Petty cash book

h Sales journal

i Cash book

j Purchases returns journal

14 a Invoice

b Till roll

c Sales invoice

d Bank statement

e Cheque counterfoil

f Paying-in-slip counterfoil

g Petty cash voucher

h Credit note (received)

i Copy of credit note

j Invoice

15 a i *Sales journal* – P Platt 288, A Lodge 800, L Fox 1560, P Platt 696, J Jackson 441, total 3785
  ii *Sales returns journal* – P Platt 96, L Fox 120, total 216

b *Sales Ledger*
Dr: P Platt 288 696, A Lodge 800, L Fox 1560, J Jackson 441
Cr: P Platt 96, L Fox 120

c *Nominal Ledger*
Dr: Sales returns 216
Cr: Sales 3785

d L Fox buys goods in larger quantities than the other customers, so he is given a higher percentage trade discount for bulk buying.

16 a Dr: Cash – Balance b/d 105, Sales 1140, Sales 1850, Total 3095, Balance b/d 1201
Dr: Bank – Balance b/d 460, Cash 1500, L Reid 2100, Paul Smith 290, Total 4350, Balance b/d 1565
Cr: Cash – Wages 220, Bank 1500, Postage 24, Drawings 150, Balance b/d 201, Total 2095
Cr: Bank – Tom Lee 740, M Lewis 75, General expenses 84, Fixtures and fittings 2830, Bank charges 56, Balance b/d 565, Total 4350

b Contra entry

c 3 Till roll, 7 Cheque counterfoil, 8 Cheque counterfoil, 9 Cheque counterfoil, 10 Till roll, 11 Paying-in-slip counterfoil, 15 Paying-in-slip counterfoil, 19 Cheque counterfoil, 20 Cash receipt, 24 Paying-in-slip counterfoil, 25 Cheque counterfoil, 26 Cash receipt, 28 Bank statement.

d Cash is a physical asset, so it is impossible to pay out more cash than is available.

17 a Dr: Discount allowed – A Chang 5, Sally Wong 62, total 67

Dr: Cash – Balance b/d 125, Sales 850, Sales 460, Total 1435, Balance b/d 305
Dr: Bank – Balance b/d 1650, A Chang 245, Cash 600, Sally Wong 3038, Total 5533, Balance b/d 1045
Cr: Discount received – Jack Black 44, P White 48, Total 92
Cr: Cash – General expenses 34, Wages 180, Bank 600, Drawings 100, Purchases 56, Insurance 160, Balance c/d 305 Total 1435
Cr: Bank – Jack Black 836, P White 1152, Equipment 1000, Loan 1500, Balance c/d 1045, Total 5533

b *Sales Ledger* Cr: A Chang 245, 5, Sally Wong 3038, 62
Purchases Ledger Dr: Jack Black 836, 44, P White 1152, 48

c *Nominal Ledger* Dr: Discount allowed 67, Cr: Discount received 92

18 a Dr: Discount allowed – R Mills 11, B Price 8, Total 19
Dr: Cash – Balance b/d 236, Sales 380, Sales 810, Sales 750, Total 2176, Balance b/d 406
Dr: Bank – R Mills 539, Interest received 60, B Price 392, Cash 1400, Balance c/d 500, Total 2891
Cr: Discount received – B Bell 14, V Slater 17, Total 31
Cr: Cash – Purchases 220, Wages 150, Bank 1400, Balance c/d 406, Total 2176
Cr: Bank – Balance b/d 420, Insurance 194, B Bell 336, V Slater 833, Electricity 108, Equipment 1000, Total 2891, Balance b/d 500

b Cash discount is given for prompt payment. Trade discount is given for bulk buying.
Cash discount is calculated on the amount due. Trade discount is calculated on the cost.
Cash discount is recorded in the accounts. Trade discount is deducted on the invoice, and is not recorded in the accounts.

19 Dr: Purchases returns 64, Bank 663, Discount received 17, Balance c/d 436, Total 1180
Cr: Balance b/d 680, Purchases 280, Purchases 220, Total 1180, Balance b/d 436

20 Dr: Balance b/d 750, Sales 464, Sales 672, Total 1886, Balance b/d 1040
Cr: Bank 735, Discount allowed 15, Sales returns 96, Balance c/d 1040, Total 1886

21 a i Dr: Equipment 6000, Motor vehicles 9500, Inventory 11 900, Cash 100, Total 27 500
Cr: Trade payables 2000, Bank overdraft 1800, Bank loan 3000, Capital 20 700, Total 27 500
Assets and liabilities at this date

ii Dr: Wages 118, Cr: Bank 118
Wages of $275 incorrectly entered in the cash book as $157

iii Dr: P Wood 4000, Cr: Equipment 4000
Sold equipment on credit to P Wood
Dr: Equipment 8000, Cr: L P Stores 8000
Bought equipment on credit from LP Stores

iv Dr: Bad debts 640, Cr: Bill Jones 640
Bad debt written off

v Dr: Bank 600, Cr: J Gibson 600
Cheque received $300 entered on the credit side of the bank account

vi Dr: Depreciation 510, Cr: Provision for depreciation of fixtures and fittings 510
Depreciation of fixtures and fittings at 15%

b The general journal is used to record any financial transaction which cannot be recorded in one of the other six specialist books of prime entry.

22 a i *General Journal*

Jan 1 Dr: Equipment 6000, Motor vehicle 12 000, Cash at bank 480, Cash in hand 150, Total 18 630
Cr: Bank loan 8000, Capital 10 630, Total 18 630
Assets and liabilities at this date

Jan 29 Dr: Equipment 500, Cr: J Carter 500
Equipment bought on credit, invoice no P74

Jan 30 Dr: Drawings 200, Cr: Purchases 200
Goods taken for private use

b *Cash Book*
Dr: Discount allowed – C Parker 18, total 18
Dr: Cash – Balance b/d 150, Sales 650, Sales 425, Total 1225, Balance b/d 50
Dr: Bank – Balance b/d 480, Cash 800, C Parker 702, Total 1982, Balance b/d 127
Cr: Discount received – P Moore 24, total 24
Cr: Cash – Purchases 230, Wages 85, Bank 800, Drawings 60, Balance c/d 50, Total 1225
Cr: Bank – General expenses 45, P Moore 1176, Bank loan 400, Rent 180, Loan interest 54,
Balance c/d 127, Total 1982

i *Purchases Journal* P Moore 1350, B Wright 672, Total 2022

ii *Purchases Returns Journal* P Moore 150, Total 150

iii *Sales Journal* A Hill 1120, C Parker 720, Total 1840

iv *Sales Returns Journal* A Hill 128, Total 128

c *Nominal Ledger*
Equipment – Dr: Balance b/d 6000, J Carter 500
Motor vehicle – Dr: Balance b/d 12 000
Bank loan – Dr: Bank 400, Cr: Balance b/d 8000
Capital – Cr: Balance b/d 10 630
J Carter – Cr: Equipment 500,
Purchases – Dr: Cash 230, Purchases journal – 2022, Cr: Drawings 200
Purchases returns – Cr: Purchases returns journal 150,
Sales Cr: Cash 650, Cash 425, Sales journal 1840
Sales returns – Dr: Sales returns journal 128,
Discount allowed Dr: Cash book 18
Wages – Dr: Cash 85,
General expenses – Dr: Bank 45,
Drawings Dr: Cash 60, Purchases 200
Rent Dr: – Bank 180,
Loan interest – Dr: Bank 54,
Discount received Cr: Cash book 24
Purchases Ledger
P Moore Dr: – Purchases returns 150, Bank 1176, Discount received 24, Cr – Purchases 1350
B Wright Cr – Purchases 672
Sales Ledger
A Hill Dr: – Sales 1120, Cr – Sales returns 128
C Parker Dr: – Sales 720 Cr – Bank 702, Discount allowed 18

d *Trial Balance at 31 January 2018*

Dr: Cash 50, Bank 127, Equipment 6500, Motor vehicle 12 000, Purchases 2052, Sales returns 128, Discount allowed 18, Wages 85, General expenses 45, Drawings 260, Rent 180, Loan interest 54, A Hill 992, Total 22 491
Cr: Bank loan 7600, Capital 10 630, J Carter 500, Purchases returns 150, Sales 2915, Discount received 24, B Wright 672, Total 22 491

23 *General Journal*

a Dr: Equipment 10 000, Fixtures and fittings 6500, Motor vehicle 8000, Inventory 4500, Cash in hand 250, Total 29 250

Cr: Trade payables 3000, Cash at bank 1500, Capital 24 750, Total 29 250

b Dr: Equipment 2300, Cr: Andrew Sharp 2300

c Dr: Shan Ltd 800, Cr: Fixtures and fittings 800

d Dr: Susan Grey 340, Cr: Brenda Grey 340

e Dr: Andrew Sharp 250, Cr: Equipment 250

f Dr: Insurance 500, Cr: Bank 500

g Dr: Bad debts 540, Cr: Soo Ling 540

h Dr: Depreciation 2200, Cr: Provision for depreciation of motor vehicles 2200

j Dr: Revenue 36 700, Cr: Income statement 36 700

k Dr: Income statement 650, Cr: Advertising 650

SECTION 3 CORRECTION OF ERRORS

Multiple Choice Questions

1 a   **2** d   **3** d   **4** b   **5** a

Shorter-Answer Questions

6 a Error of commission – where a debit or credit entry is made for the correct amount in the correct class of account, but in the wrong account.

Error of principle – where a debit or credit entry is made for the correct amount but in the wrong class of account.

b Error of omission – where a transaction is completely omitted from the records.

Error of original entry – where a mistake is made transferring the amount from the source document to the subsidiary book.

7 An error of original entry does not affect the balancing of the trial balance because both the debit and credit entries will be the same even though they are the wrong figure.

8 A suspense account is a temporary account to be used when the trial balance totals do not agree. The difference will be debited or credited to the suspense account.

9 Debit bank account $400; credit Ayre Ltd sales ledger account $400.

Longer-Answer Questions

10 a **i.** Error of commission; **ii.** Error of omission; **iii.** Error of commission; **iv.** Error of principle; **v.** Error of original entry

b **i**   Debit Motor repair 480, Credit Rent and rates 480

　　ii   Debit Insurance 1260, Credit Bank account 1260

　　iii   Debit T Rodgerson account 415, Credit T Rodgers account 415

　　iv   Debit Plant and machinery 1450, Credit Repairs and maintenance 1450

　　v   Debit Paper Supplies account 9, Credit Stationery 9.

11 a **i**   Debit Sales 200, Credit Suspense account 200

　　ii   Debit Suspense account 130, Credit Interest received 130

　　iii   Debit Postage 25, Credit Suspense account 25

　　iv   Debit Suspense account 105, Credit G Boyd sales ledger account 105

b Debit Balance b/d 200; Interest received 130; Total 330

Credit Sales 200; Postage 25, G Boyd 105; Total 330

12 a Debit Repairs 440, Credit Suspense account 440
Debit Suspense account 100, Credit Sales 100
Debit Suspense account 290, Credit Zac Charles account 290

  b Debit Balance b/d (balance) 50; Sales 100; Zac Charles 290; Total 440
Credit Repairs 440; Total 440

13 a Debit Evans sales ledger account 360, Credit Evison sales ledger account 360
Debit Discounts received 200, Credit Suspense account 200
Debit Bank account 360, Credit Interest received 360
Debit Motor repairs 20, Credit Suspense account 20

  b Debit Balance b/d 220; Total 220
Credit Discounts received 200; Motor repairs 20; Total 220

14 a Debit Heat and light 440, Credit Bank account 440
Debit Purchases returns 300, Credit Suspense account 300
Debit David Bishop account 380, Credit David Barton account 380
Debit Cash account 450, Credit Sales 450
Debit Suspense account 90, Credit Stationery 90

  b Debit Balance b/d 210; Stationery 90; Total 300
Credit Purchases returns 300; Total 300

15 Profit per income statement 38 300 + Rent 2500 − Revenue 1900 − Depreciation 4800 − Advertising 300 = Revised profit 33 800

16 Loss per income statement (2700) + Discount received 1400 + Heat and light 500 + Revenue 13 600 − Bank interest 800 + Rent 4500 = Revised profit 16 500

17 Non-current assets 55 000

Current assets: Inventory 5000 (10 000 − 5000) +Trade receivables 10 000 (13 000 − 3000) + Other receivables 5000 (3000 + 2000) + Bank 8000 = 28 000

Total assets 83 000

Capital: Opening balance 42 000 + Profit for the year 38 000 (46 000 − 5000 − 3000) − Drawings 28 000 = 52 000

Current liabilities: Trade payables 26 000 + Other payables 5000 (4000 + 1000) = 31 000

Total Capital and liabilities 83 000

SECTION 4 VERIFICATION: BANK RECONCILIATION AND CONTROL ACCOUNTS

Multiple Choice Questions

1 c   **2** b   **3** b   **4** d

Shorter-Answer Questions: Bank Reconciliation

5 *Bank reconciliation statement*

Balance as per cash book 1898, add unpresented cheques 537, subtotal 2435, less uncredited bankings 914, balance as per bank statement 1521

6 *Bank reconciliation statement*

Balance as per bank statement 259, less unpresented cheques 719, subtotal overdrawn 460, add uncredited bankings 672, balance as per cash book 212

7 Direct debit: authority is given to a bank by one of its customers to make payments on its behalf to another organisation. The amount paid to the organisation will be up to a specified limit.

Standing order: authority is given to a bank by one of its customers to make payments of a fixed amount at regular individuals to another organisation.

8 Two from: helping to identify errors in the cash book and/or bank statement; enables the cash book to be kept up to date with transactions which have so far only been recorded by the bank; helps reduce the chance of fraud because there is an external check on the business's records.

Shorter-Answer Questions: Control Accounts

9 A purchases ledger account could have a debit balance because a supplier has been overpaid/ goods have been returned to a supplier after the account has been settled.

10 Checks the arithmetical accuracy of the sales ledger; provides a fast means of finding a total of trade receivables for use in financial statements; helps prevent fraud because the sales ledger is subject to regular checks.

11 Discounts received; payments to Trade payables

12 Cheques received from Trade receivables now dishonoured; Credit sales

Longer-Answer Questions: Bank Reconciliation

13 a *Cash book update*

Dr: Opening balance 5161, Credit transfer C Thomas 390

Cr: DD Regional Telecoms 220, Charges 54, Closing balance c/d 5277

(Note: the closing balance b/d will appear as a debit entry)

b *Bank reconciliation statement (version 1)*

Balance as per cash book 5277, add unpresented cheques (833; 1380) 2213, less amount not yet credited 1230, balance as per bank statement 6260

b *Bank reconciliation statement (version 2)*

Balance as per bank statement 6260, less unpresented cheques 2313, add amount not yet credited 1230, balance as per cash book 5277

14 a *Cash book update*

Dr: Opening balance 2382, Credit transfer 441

Cr: Bank charges 84, SO Rent 485, Drawings 18, Balance c/d 2236

(Note: the closing balance b/d will appear as a debit entry)

b *Bank reconciliation statement (version 1)*

Balance as per cash book 2236, add unpresented cheque 332, less amount not yet credited 1432, add error in bank statement 132, balance as per bank statement 1268

b *Bank reconciliation statement (version 2)*

Balance as per bank statement 1268, less error in bank statement 132, less unpresented cheques 332, add amount not yet credited 1432, balance as per cash book 2236

15 a The bank columns in the cash book are an asset in the business's books; the payment is a decrease in an asset account; a decrease in an asset is recorded as a credit entry according to the rules of double-entry. The customer's account in the bank's books is a liability; the payment by the customer decreases the liability; a decrease in a liability is recorded as a debit entry according to the rules of double-entry.

b *Cash book update*

Dr: Credit transfer 480, Balance c/d 2217

Cr: Opening balance 2360, Charges 139, error Sales 198

(Note: the closing balance b/d will appear as a credit entry)

c The updated balance of 2217 should be shown in the statement of financial position as a current liability.

d *Bank reconciliation statement (version 1)*

Balance as per cash book (overdrawn) 2217, Unpresented cheques (1397; 300) 1697, Subtotal overdraft 520, Amount not credited 375, Balance as per bank statement 895 (overdrawn)

d *Bank reconciliation statement (version 2)*

Balance as per bank statement (overdrawn) 895, unpresented cheques (1397; 300) 1697, subtotal overdraft 2592, amount not credited 375, balance as per cash book 2217 (overdrawn)

Longer-Answer Questions: Control Accounts

16 a *Purchases ledger control account*

Dr Discounts received 472, Payments 14 950, Returns out 589, Closing balance c/d 9236

Cr: Opening balance 8920, Purchases 16 327

(Note: the closing balance b/d will appear as a credit entry)

b *Sales ledger control account*

Dr: Opening balance 11 430, Sales 20 445

Cr: Discounts allowed 880, Receipts 22 748, Returns in 491, Closing balance c/d 7756

(Note: the closing balance b/d will appear as a debit entry)

17 *Sales ledger control account*

Dr: Opening balance 23 786, Dishonoured cheques 827, Credit sales 85 492, Interest charges 256, Refunds 163, Closing balance c/d 620

Cr: Opening balance 1034, Irrecoverable debts 2824, Contra 440, Discounts allowed 3721, Receipts 82 142, Returns in 3462, Closing balance c/d 17 521

(Note: the closing balance of 17 521 will appear as a debit entry; the closing balance of 620 will appear as a credit entry)

18 a *Purchases ledger control account*

Dr: Opening balance 414, Contra 620, Discounts received 561, Payments 24 372, Returns out 1927, Closing balance c/d 4507

Cr: Opening balance 8450, Purchases 23 726, Closing balance c/d 225

(Note: the closing balance of 225 will appear as a debit entry; the closing balance of 4507 will appear as a credit entry)

b The conclusions are that there are errors in the accounts. These could be in the Purchases ledger, the Purchases ledger control account, or both.

c Credit sales debit entry; discounts allowed credit entry; returns outwards no entry; contra credit entry.

SECTION 5 PREPARING FINANCIAL STATEMENTS

Multiple Choice Questions

1 c **2** b **3** c **4** d **5** d **6** b **7** a **8** c **9** c **10** c

Shorter-Answer Questions: Adjustments for Other Payables and Other Receivables

11 Administration expenses 3690 (3420 + 270)
Insurance 1688 (1812 − 124)
Interest on bank loan 790 (740 + 50)
Rent 8760 (9440 − 620)

12 a Electricity charges 2140 (1930 + 210); Interest received on loan 585 (475 + 110);
General expenses 536 (626 − 90); Rent received 5180 (5420 − 240)

b Current assets: Interest 110, General expenses 90

c Current liabilities: Electricity charges 210, Rent 240

13 a Water charges 2850 (−360 + 2730 + 480)

b Dr: Bank 2730, Closing balance c/d 480
Cr: Opening balance b/d 360, Income statement 2850
(Note the Closing balance b/d 480 is a credit entry)

14 a Rent received 5280 (−530 + 6300 − 490)

b Dr: Opening balance b/d 530, Income statement 5280, Closing balance c/d 490
Cr: Bank 6300
(Note the Closing balance b/d is a credit entry)

Shorter-Answer Questions: Depreciation and Disposal of Non-Current Assets

15 a 1950 (Forecast loss in value 7800/4)

b 4500 (Cost less depreciation for two years, i.e. 3900)

c Dr: 2019 Balance c/d 3900
Cr: 2018 Income statement 1950
Cr: 2019 Income statement 1950
(Note the Closing balance b/d is a credit entry of 3900)

16 a 2880 (Depreciation year 1 20% ×18 000, i.e. 3600 nbv 14 400; Depreciation year 2 20% ×14 400)

b 11 520 (i.e.18 000 less year 1 Depreciation 3600 and less year 2 Depreciation 2880)

17 a 1020 (i.e. Opening balance 4750 plus Additions 890, i.e. 5640 less Closing valuation 4620)

b Dr: Opening balance b/d 4750, Bank 890
Cr: Income statement 1020, Closing balance c/d 4620
(Note the Closing balance b/d is a debit entry)

18 Technological change; inadequacy; time factor

19 a Profit 1100 (i.e. 29 500 less Depreciation 23 400, i.e. nbv 6100; Proceeds 7200 less nbv)

   b Dr: Cost 29 500, Income statement (profit) 1100
   Cr: Depreciation 23 400, Bank 7200

Shorter-Answer Questions: Irrecoverable Debts and Provisions for Doubtful Debts

20 Dr: Income statement 860; Cr: Provision for doubtful debts 860

21 Dr: Income statement 60; Cr: Provision for doubtful debts 60

22 a Dr: Provision for doubtful debts 114; Cr: Income statement 114

   b Current assets: Trade receivables 36 200 less Provision for doubtful debts 724, net 35 476

Shorter-Answer Questions: Capital and Revenue Expenditure and Receipts

23 a Payments which are of long-term benefit to a business (more than one year), i.e. payments to acquire non-current assets.

   b Payments which are of short-term benefit to a business (less than one year), i.e. payments for running costs such as wages.

24 a Receipts which are of long-term benefit to a business (more than one year) such as amounts invested by the owner of a business or a long-term loan.

   b Receipts which are of short-term benefit to a business (less than one year) such as receipts from sales of goods or from providing a service.

25 a Profit will be overstated by the amount of the loan.

   b The business's capital will be overstated on the statement of financial position because profit for the year has been overstated; non-current liabilities will be understated because the loan will be omitted.

Longer-Answer Questions: Adjustments for Other Payables and Other Receivables; Depreciation and Disposal of Non-Current Assets

26 *Income statement*

Revenue 162 330 less Cost of sales [Opening inventory 9490 + Purchases 49 200 (i.e. Purchases 49 440 less Goods own use 240) + Carriage inwards 620 − Closing inventory 3980] 55 330, Gross profit 107 000 add Rent received (2290 − in advance 280) 2010 less Expenses [General expenses 780 + Insurance (1120 − Prepaid 110) 1010 + Loan interest 730 + Property taxes 650 + Wages (31 110 + due 1200) 32 310 + Depreciation equipment 3000 + Depreciation premises 2806] 41 286; Profit for the year 67 724

Statement of financial position

Non-current assets: Premises (cost 140 300 less Depreciation 16 836) nbv 123 464 + Equipment (cost 16 000 less Depreciation 7000) nbv 9000; Subtotal 132 464

Current assets: Inventory 3980, Trade receivables 4800, Other receivables 110, Bank 2330; Subtotal 11 220

Capital: Opening balance 77 100 + Profit for year 67 724 − Drawings (17 580 + Goods for own use 240) 17 820; Subtotal 127 004

Non-current liability: Bank loan 8000

Current liabilities: Trade payables 7200, Other payables (Wages 1200 + Rent received in advance 280) 1480; Subtotal 8680

Totals: 143 684

27 *Income statement*

Gross profit 84 910 add Rent received (8430 − in advance 820 + due 390) 8000 less Expenses [Administration expenses (4410 + due 130) 4540 + Carriage outwards 820 + Insurance (1680 − Prepaid 240) 1440 + Loss on disposal of motor vehicle 430 + Wages and salaries (34 860 + due 730) 35 590 + Depreciation furniture and equipment (nbv 12 800 × 20%) 2560 + Depreciation premises (240 000 × 2%) 4800] 50 180; Profit for the year 42 730

Statement of financial position

Non-current assets: Premises (Cost 240 000 less Depreciation 24 000) nbv 216 000 + Furniture and equipment (Cost 20 000 less Depreciation 9760) nbv 10 240; Subtotal 226 240

Current assets: Inventory 17 450, Trade receivables 14 450, Other receivables (Insurance 240; Rent received 390) 630; Subtotal 32 530

Capital: Opening balance 223 000 + Profit for the year 42 730 − Drawings 21 770; Subtotal 243 960

Current liabilities: Trade payables 11 420, Other payables (Wages and salaries 730 + Rent received in advance 820 + Administration 130) 1680; Bank 1710; Subtotal 14 810

Totals: 258 770

Longer-Answer Questions: Bad Debts and Provisions for Doubtful Debts

28 *Income statement*

Revenue (106 481 less Returns inwards 827) 105 654 less Cost of sales [Opening inventory 4847 + Purchases net 49 405 (i.e. Purchases 49 371 less Returns outwards 238 plus Carriage inwards 272) − Closing inventory 3922] Total: 50 330

Gross profit 55 324 add Income [Debts written off recovered 120 + Interest received (392 + due 120) 512 + Discounts received 448] 1080 less Expenses [Irrecoverable debts 494 + Carriage outwards 118 + Discounts allowed 327 + Electricity (1873 + due 189) 2062 + General expenses 1020 + Rent 12 391 + Wages 12 272 + Water charges (994 − Prepaid 116) 878 + Depreciation vehicles (21 200 × 25%) 5300 + Provision for doubtful debts (12 400 × 4%) 496] Total: 35 360; Profit for the year 21 044

29 *Income statement*

Revenue 174 360 less Cost of sales [Opening inventory 27 650 + Purchases 82 980 − Closing inventory 31 350] 79 280, Gross profit 95 080 add Income (Profit on disposal of furniture 240 + Discounts received 370) 610 less Expenses [Advertising (3400 − Prepaid 480) 2920 + Bank loan interest 940 + Insurance 2230 + Rent 11 480 + Wages (44 100 + due 1820) 45 920 + Depreciation furniture and equipment (17 800 × 15%) 2670 + Depreciation motor vehicles (nbv 23 040 × 20%) 4608 + increase in Provision for doubtful debts (18 200 × 4% less Existing provision 640) 88] Total: 70 856; Profit for year 24 834

Statement of financial position

Non-current assets: Motor vehicles (cost 36 000 less Depreciation 17 568) nbv 18 432 + Furniture and equipment (cost 17 800 less Depreciation 11 070) nbv 6730; Subtotal 25 162

Current assets: Inventory 31 350, Trade receivables (18 200 less Provision for doubtful debts 728) 17 472, Other receivables 480, Bank 7250; Subtotal 56 552

Capital: Opening balance 65 000 + Profit for the year 24 834 − Drawings 32 410; Subtotal 57 424

Non-current liability: Bank loan 12 500

Current liabilities: Trade payables 9970, Other payables 1820; Subtotal 11 790

Total: 81 714

Longer-Answer Questions: Capital and Revenue Expenditure and Receipts

30 a Revenue expenditure items: wages of coach drivers, repairs to coach, interest on bank loan.

Capital expenditure items: extension to garage buildings, new coach, business logo added to new coach.

Revenue receipts: received from customers for coach trips.

Capital receipts: sold coach; bank loan; Leon paid some of his private funds into business.

b The distinction is important because otherwise the business's profit will not be calculated accurately and the figures for non-current assets, non-current liabilities and capital will be incorrect on the business's statement of financial position. For example, assets will be understated if the purchase of the coach was included in the income statement, profit would be understated too. If these key figures are inaccurate it is likely that decision-making will be affected because key data is wrong. Poor decision-making will have an adverse effect on the business's performance.

31 *Profit for the year*

Revenue 125 610 add Income [Rent received (1850 − 290 in advance) 1560 + decrease in Provision for doubtful debts (210 −140) 70] 1630 less Expenses [Irrecoverable debts 120, Insurance (8320 − prepaid 190) 8130 + Motor vehicle running costs 11 490 + Motor vehicle repairs 3940 + Office expenses (840 + 140 due) 980 + Wages and salaries 25 360 + depreciation Premises 6900 + depreciation Furniture and equipment (6300 × 20%) 1260 + depreciation Motor vehicles (nbv 76 000 × 20%)]
73 380; Profit for year 53 860

Statement of financial position

Non-current assets: Goodwill 30 000 + Premises [cost 230 000 + 9000 air conditioning, i.e. 239 000 less depreciation 13 800) 225 200 + Motor vehicles (cost 95 000 less depreciation 34 200) nbv 60 800 + Furniture and equipment (cost 6300 less depreciation 2520) nbv 3780; subtotal 319 780

Current assets: Trade receivables (4800 less Provision for doubtful debts 140) 4660, Other receivables 190; Subtotal 4850

Capital: Opening balance 300 000 + Profit for the year 53 860 − Drawings 31 330; Subtotal 322 530

Current liabilities: Trade payables 880, Other payables (Rent in advance 290 + Office expenses due 140) 430, Bank 790; Subtotal 2100

Totals: 324 630

SECTION 6 PARTNERSHIP ACCOUNTS

Multiple Choice Questions

1 a   **2** b   **3** b   **4** b

Shorter-Answer Questions

5 Interest on capital, interest on drawings, partnership salary, share of loss

6 Debit: drawings, interest on drawings, share of loss
Credit: interest on capital, interest on a partner's loan, partnership salary

7 a Two from: May be able to share responsibilities for running the business, easing the workload; be able to make use of specialist expertise of each partner.

b One from: possibility of disagreements, decision-making may take longer, business may be short-lived (if partner retires or dies).

8 Four from details of: partnership salaries, interest on capital, interest on drawings, interest on partnership loan, limits on drawings, each partner's responsibilities, amount of capital to be invested.

9 Pamela 67 000. Workings: salary 15 000 + interest on capital (10% × 80 000) 8000 + share of residual profit (see below: 4/9 × 99 000) 44 000

Robin 66 000. Workings: interest on capital (10% × 110 000) 11 000 + share of residual profits (see below 5/9 × 99 000) 55 000

Residual profit is profit for year 133 000 less salary 15 000 less interest on capital total 19 000, i.e. 99 000.

10 Ahmed net share 35 600. Workings: interest on drawings 2000, share of residual loss (see below 3/5 × 56 000) 33 600

Bamber net share 3400. Workings: interest on drawings 3000, partnership salary 22 000, residual loss (see below 2/5 × 56 000) 22 400

Residual loss is loss for year 39 000 add interest on drawings 5000 (subtotal 34 000) less salary 22 000, i.e. 56 000

Longer-Answer Questions

11 *Appropriation account for the year ended 30 November 2018*
Profit for the year 74 000 less partnership salary (Emilie) 8000 (subtotal 66 000); less interest on capitals (Emilie: 8% × 80 000, i.e. 6400) (Marco: 8% × 50 000, i.e. 4000) 10 400 (subtotal 55 600); less shares of residual profit (Emilie: 3/5 × 55 600, i.e. 33 360) (Marco: 2/5 × 55 600, i.e. 22 240)

12 a *Residual profit*: profit for the year 38 600 add interest on drawings 1460, less salary 18 000, less interest on capitals 15 600, i.e. 6460

Each partner's share of residual profit is 3230.

b *Current accounts*

Rakesh

Dr: Opening balance 4500, interest on drawings 640, drawings 16 000, closing balance c/d 8290

Cr : salary 18 000, interest on capital 8200, residual profit 3230

Vikash

Dr: interest on drawings 820, drawings 20 500

Cr: opening balance 6200, interest on capital 7400, residual profit 3230, closing balance c/d 4490

c Rakesh is owed 8290 by the partnership; Vikash owes the partnership 4490.

13 *Workings – shares or profit:*

Amanda: interest on capital (10% × 60 000) 6000 plus share of residual profit (31 400 × ½) 15 700

Sylvia: interest on capital (10% × 50 000) 5000 plus share of residual profit 15 700

Statement of financial position at 31 December 2018

Non-current assets 87 300

Current assets – Inventory 14 200, Trade receivables 8300, Other receivables 700, Bank 3200; Subtotal 26 400, Total 113 700

Capital *accounts* – Amanda 60 000, Sylvia 50 000, Subtotal 110 000

Current accounts – Amanda: Opening balance (600), Interest on capital 6000, Residual profit 15 700, Drawings (21 200), Net (100)

Sylvia: Opening balance 2500, Interest on capital 5000, Residual profit 15 700, Drawings (26 500), Net (3300), Subtotal (3400)

Current liabilities – trade payables 6500, other payables 600; subtotal 7100, Total 113 700

14 *Income statement for the year ended 30 September 2018*

Revenue 139 910 less Returns in 830, Net 139 080; less Cost of sales – Opening inventory 14 440 plus Purchases 83 450 less Closing inventory 11 250, i.e. 86 640;

Gross profit 52 440 less Administration expenses 3640, Carriage outwards 1430, Depreciation of furniture [20% × (50 000 – 18 000)] 6400, Insurance (3410 less prepaid 290) 3120, Loan interest for Samir (18 000 × 5%) 900, Wages (29 620 plus due 430) 30 050, i.e. Total expenses 45 540, Profit for the year 6900

Appropriation account for the year ended 30 September 2018

Profit for year 6900 add Interest on drawings (Kalpa, 10% × 23 200) 2320, (Samir, 10% × 17 800) 1780 (subtotal 11 000) less Interest on capitals (Kalpa, 8% × 90 000) 7200 (Samir, 8% × 70 000) 5600 (subtotal loss 1800) less Salary 15 000 (subtotal loss 16 800) less Shares of residual loss (Kalpa 8400, Samir 8400)

SECTION 7 LIMITED COMPANY ACCOUNTS

Multiple Choice Questions

1 c   **2** c   **3** c   **4** a

Shorter-Answer Questions

5 a Shareholders are the owners of a limited company. Directors are appointed by the shareholders to manage the company on their behalf.

  b Ordinary shares have voting rights and the shareholders receive a variable amount of dividend depending on the profits available for distribution. Preference shares do not generally have voting rights and the holders receive a fixed rate of dividend.

6 a Retained earnings are the accumulated profits of the company that have not been used to pay dividends or that have not been transferred to a general reserve.

  b General reserve is that part of the undistributed profits that have been set aside for some future use.

7 Ordinary share dividend = 50 000 × 0.25 = 12 500 × 5% = $625.

8 Preference share dividend = 80 000 × 8% = 6400
Ordinary share dividend = 300 000 shares × 5c = 15 000
Total dividends = $21 400

9 Preference share dividend = 200 000 × 6% = $12 000
Ordinary share dividend = 400 000 shares × 50c = 200 000 × 5% = $10 000

10 *R Ltd. Income statement for the year ended 30 November 2018*
Revenue 842 000 − Cost of sales 352 000 (93 000 + 365 000 − 106 000) = Gross profit 490 000 − Operating expenses 203 000 ((84 000 − 3000) + (280 000 × 20%) + 66 000) = Operating profit 287 000 − Finance charges 7000 (4000 + 3000) = Profit for the year 280 000.

11 *S Ltd. Income statement for the year ended 30 September 2018*
Revenue 615 000 − cost of sales 288 000 (62 000 + 285 000 − 59 000) = gross profit 327 000 − operating expenses 211 100 (152 250 − 3250 +(80 000 × 15%) +1600 + 48 500) = operating profit 115 900 − finance charges 7500 (2025 + 675 + 2400 + 2400) = profit for the year 108 400.

12 *B Ltd. Statement of changes in equity for the year ended 30 June 2018*
Share capital; b/f 150 000 = c/f 150 000
Retained earnings: b/f 146 000 + Profit for the year 85 000 − Dividends paid 18 000 − Transfer to general reserve 40 000 = c/f 173 000
General reserve: b/f 26 000 + Transfer from retained earnings 40 000 = c/f 66 000
Total: 322 000 + 85 000 − 18 000 = 389 000

13 *S Ltd. Statement of changes in equity for the year ended 30 September 2018*
Share capital; b/f 125 000 = c/f 125 000

Retained earnings: b/f 12 000 + Profit for the year 62 000 − Dividends paid 37 500 − Transfer to general reserve 20 000 = c/f 16 500

General reserve: b/f 60 000 + Transfer from retained earnings 20 000 = c/f 80 000

Total: 197 000 + 62 000 − 37 500 = 221 500

14 *G Ltd. Statement of financial position at 30 June 2018*

Non-current assets: 362 600 (465 000 − 102 400)

Current assets: Inventory 63 500 + Trade receivables 27 000 + Other receivables 3200 + Bank 14 900 = 108 600

Total assets: 362 600 + 108 600 = 471 200

Capital and reserves

Share capital: Ordinary shares 200 000 + 6% Preference shares 150 000 + Retained earnings 65 400 = 415 400

Current liabilities: Trade payables 14 600 + Other payables 1200 = 15 800

Non-current liabilities: 6% Debentures 40 000

Total capital and liabilities 415 400 + 15 800 + 40 000 = 471 200

15 *S Ltd. Statement of financial position at 31 March 2018*

Non-current assets: 316 000 − 122 600 = 193 400

Current assets: Inventory 42 300 + Trade receivables (38 200 − 900) 37 300 + Other receivables 5800 = 85 400

Total assets: 193 400 + 85 400 = 278 800

Capital and reserves

Share capital: Ordinary shares 120 000 + 5% Preference shares 90 000 + Retained earnings 21 900 = 231 900

Current liabilities: Trade payables 22 400 + Other payables 1600 + Bank (4300 − 1400) 2900 = 26 900

Non-current liabilities: 8% Debentures 20 000

Total capital and liabilities 231 900 + 26 900 + 20 000 = 278 800

16 a *M Ltd. Income statement for the year ended 31 July 2018*

Revenue 448 200 − Cost of sales (42 800 + 212 600 − 49 200) 206 200 = Gross profit 242 000 − Operating expenses [(115 300 − 4500 + 300) 159 100 + 48 000)] = Operating profit 82 900 − Finance charges (2400 + 2400) 4800 = Profit for the year 78 100

b *M Ltd. Statement of changes in equity for the year ended 31 July 2018*

Ordinary share capital; b/f 200 000 = c/f 200 000

Preference share capital: b/f 80 000 = c/f 80 000

Retained earnings: b/f 29 000 + Profit for the year 78 100 − Dividends paid 12 000 = c/f 95 100

General reserve: b/f 22 000 = c/f 22 000

Total: 200 000 + 80 000 + 95 100 + 22 000 = 397 100

c *M Ltd. Statement of financial position at 31 July 2018*

Non-current assets: 375 000 − 63 000 = 312 000

Current assets: Inventory 49 200 + Trade receivables (39 100 − 900) 38 200 + Other receivables (4700 + 4500) 9200 + Bank 8900 = 105 500

Total assets: (312 000 + 105 500) = 417 500

Capital and reserves

Share capital: Ordinary shares 200 000 + 6% Preference shares 80 000 + Retained earnings 95 100 + General reserve 22 000 = 397 100

Current liabilities: Trade payables 16 900 + Other payables (1100 + 2400) 3500 = 20 400

Total capital and liabilities 397 100 + 20 400 = 417 500

17 a *R Ltd. Income statement for the year ended 30 April 2018*

Revenue 638 100 − Cost of sales (53 000 + 324 000 − 61 000) 316 000 = Gross profit 322 100 − Operating expenses (185 700 − 200 + 62 000) 247 500 = Operating profit 74 600 − Finance charges (3500 + 3500) 7000 = Profit for the year 67 600.

b *R Ltd. Statement of changes in equity for the year ended 30 April 2018*

Ordinary share capital; b/f 140 000 = c/f 140 000

Preference share capital: b/f 250 000 = c/f 250 000

Retained earnings: b/f 106 500 + Profit for the year 67 600 − Dividends paid 25 000 = c/f 149 100

General reserve: b/f 30 000 = c/f 30 000

Total: 526 500 + 67 600 − 25 000 = 569 100

c *R Ltd. Statement of financial position at 30 April 2018*

Non-current assets: 632 000 − 140 000 = 492 000

Current assets: Inventory 61 000 + Trade receivables 71 500 (72 800 − 1300) + Other receivables 2200 = 134 700

Total assets: 492 000 + 134 700 = 626 700

Capital and reserves

Share capital: Ordinary shares 140 000 + 5% Preference shares 250 000 + Retained earnings 149 100 + General reserve 30 000 = 569 100

Current liabilities: Trade payables 39 900 + Other payables (3000 + 3500) 6500 + Bank (12 600 − 1400) 11 200 = 57 600

Total capital and liabilities 569 100 + 57 600 = 626 700

SECTION 8 CLUBS AND SOCIETIES

Multiple Choice Questions

1 d   **2** d   **3** b   **4** b   **5** b   **6** a

Shorter-Answer Questions

7 *Statement of affairs at 1 April 2018*

Assets: Equipment 7200, Fixtures and fittings 2320, Inventory 420, Subscriptions in arrears 190, Bank 650, Total 10 780

Less Liabilities: Members' loans 2500, Trade payables 270, Subscriptions in advance 140, Total 2910

Accumulated fund 7870

8 a *Subscriptions account*

Dr: Balance b/d 150, Income and expenditure 3625, Balance c/d 100, Total 3875, Balance b/d 200

Cr: Balance b/d 75, Cash 3600, Balance c/d 200, Total 3875, Balance b/d 100

b Income and expenditure account – Income (Cr) – Subscriptions 3625

9 a *Shop account*

Revenue 22 000, less Cost of sales: Opening inventory 1500, add Purchases 16 450 (16 300 − 300 + 450), less Closing inventory 1800 = 16 150, Gross profit 5850

Gross profit, less Expenses – Wages 2200, Shop expenses 540 = Profit for the year 3110

b Income and expenditure account – Income (cr) – Shop profit 3110

10 *Receipts and payments account*

Dr: Balance b/d 810, Subscriptions 4250, Competition fees 560, Bank loan 1000, Sales of refreshments 2800, Total 9420, Balance b/d 480

Cr: Equipment 3200, Competition prizes 400, Purchases of refreshments 1850, Maintenance of ground 2300, Insurance 450, General expenses 740, Balance c/d 480, Total 9420

Longer-Answer Questions

11 a *Subscriptions account*

Dr: Balance b/d 125, Income and expenditure 12 670, Balance c/d 40, Total 12 835, Balance b/d 250

Cr: Balance b/d 85, Cash 12 500, Balance c/d 250, Total 12 835, Balance b/d 40

b *Income and expenditure account for the year ended 31 December 2018*

Income: Subscriptions 12 670, Refreshments 530 (1630 −1100), Total 13 200

Less Expenditure: General expenses 3780 (3730 − 250 + 300), Insurance 2150 (2200 + 440 − 490), Secretary's expenses 1620, Depreciation: Equipment 800, Clubhouse 500, Total 8850

Surplus of income over expenditure: 4350

c *Statement of financial position at 31 December 2018*

Non-current assets: Clubhouse 14 500, Equipment 7200 (4200 + 3800 − 800), Total 21 700

Add Current assets: Bank 4230, Other receivables 740 (subscriptions in arrears 250 + insurance 490), Total 4970

Total assets 26 670

Accumulated fund:

Opening balance 18 780, add Surplus income over expenditure 4350, add Donation 400, Total 23 530

Add non-current liabilities: Members' loans 2800

Add current liabilities: Other payables 340 (General expenses 300 + Subscriptions in advance 40), Total 340

Total accumulated fund plus liabilities: 26 670

12 a *Statement of affairs at 1 January 2018*

Assets: Equipment 10 500, Inventory 180, Bank 2100, Subscriptions in arrears 240, Total 13 020

Less Liabilities: Trade payables 300, Subscriptions in advance 85, Total 385

Accumulated fund: 12 635

b *Refreshments account*

Revenue 5550, less Cost of sales: Opening inventory 180, add Purchases (2300 − 300 + 200) 2200, less Closing inventory 220 = 2160.

Gross profit 3390

Gross profit 3390 less Depreciation equipment (10 500 + 9500 = 20 000 × 10% = 2000 × 25%) = 500, Wages 1000 = Profit for the year 1890

c *Subscriptions account*

Dr: Balance b/d 240, Income and expenditure 28 420, Balance c/d 105, Total 28 765, Balance b/d 180

Cr: Balance b/d 85, Cash 28,500, Balance c/d 180, Total 28 765, Balance b/d 105

d *Income and expenditure account for the year ended 31 December 2018*

Income: Profit on refreshments 1890, Subscriptions 28 420, Donation 800, Total 31 110

Less Expenditure: Wages (18 000 − 1000) 17 000, Insurance (2025 − 225) 1800, Tennis courts (maintenance 3860 − fees 3600) 260, General expenses (820 + 80) 900, Depreciation equipment (2000 × 75%) 1500, Total 21 460

Surplus income over expenditure: 9650

e *Statement of financial position at 31 December 2018*

Non-current assets: Equipment (20 000 − 2000) 18 000

Add Current assets: Inventory 220, Bank 4045, Other receivables 405 (subscriptions in arrears 180, insurance 225) Total 4670.

Total assets 22 670

Accumulated fund

Opening balance 12 635, add Surplus income over expenditure 9650, Total 22 285

Add Current liabilities: Trade payables 200, Other payables 185 (general expenses 80 + subscriptions in advance 105) Total 385

Total accumulated fund plus liabilities: 22 670

SECTION 9 MANUFACTURING ACCOUNTS

Multiple Choice Questions

1 c   **2** b   **3** b   **4** a

Shorter-Answer Questions

5 A business produces a manufacturing account to accumulate the total costs of manufacture. This enables the business to know whether it is cheaper to manufacture or to buy products in.

6 Work in progress is the costs that are tied up in unfinished goods. Opening work in progress is added to the cost of manufacture because it has been completed in this current accounting period. Closing work in progress is deducted from the cost of manufacture because the goods will not be completed until the next accounting period.

7 Prime cost = 82 600 + 46 200 – 49 700 + 415 300 = 494 400

8 Cost of production = 225 000 + 87 400 + 14 600 – 18 300 = 308 700

Longer-Answer Questions

9 *Opening inventory*: Raw materials 26 700 + Purchases 148 600 – Closing inventory 29 500 = 145 800 (raw materials consumed) + Direct wages 34 200 = 180 000 (Prime cost) + 91 300 (Total factory overheads: 8600 + 11 300 + 48 000 + 12 100 + 7400 + 3900) = 271 300 (Cost of production).

10 *Makumba & Co. Manufacturing account for the year ended 30 September 2018*
Opening inventory: Raw materials 21 100 + Purchases 163 840 – Closing inventory 28 250 = 156 690 (Raw materials consumed) + Direct wages 65 360 = 222 050 (Prime cost) + 89 700 (Total factory overheads: 26 500 (24 380 + 2120) + 34 200 (36 600 – 2400) + 9450 (12 600 × 75%) + 11 600 (14 500 × 80%) + 1280 + 6670) = 311 750 + 4680 (opening WIP) – 5230 (closing WIP) = 311 200 (Cost of production)

11 a *Justin. Manufacturing account for the year ended 30 June 2018*
Opening inventory: Raw materials18 700 + Purchases 188 650 – Closing inventory 15 300 = 192 050 (Raw materials consumed) + Direct wages 83 420 = 275 470 (Prime cost) + 113 760 [Total factory overheads: 8290 + 18 400 + 42 090 +11 400 (15 200 × 3/4) + 9800 (12 250 × 4/5) + 4580 + 19 200 (24 000 × 4/5)] = 389 230 + 2200 (Opening WIP) – 3950 (Closing WIP) = 387 480 (Cost of production)

b *Justin. Income statement for the year ended 30 June 2018*
Revenue 593 200 – 385 180 (Cost of sales: 9100 + 387 480 – 11 400) = 208 020 (Gross profit) – 75 390 (Total overheads: 12 120 + 2550 + 6760 + 3800 (15 200 × 1/4) + 2450 (12 250 × 1/5) + 4800 (24 000 × 1/5) + 42 910) = 132 630 (Profit for the year)

12 a *Davison & Co. Manufacturing account for the year ended 31 May 2018*
Opening inventory: Raw materials 12 700 + Purchases 139 280 – Closing inventory 9800 = 142 180 (Raw materials consumed) + Direct wages 214 180 = 356 360 (Prime cost) + 163 770 (Total factory overheads: 46 730 + 28 660 + 13 500 [(24 400 – 6400) × 75%) + 9920 (49 600 × 20%) + 64 960 (81 200 × 80%)] = 520 130 + 9600 (Opening WIP) – 12 200 (Closing WIP) = 517 530 (Cost of production)

b *Davison & Co. Income statement for the year ended 31 May 2018*

Revenue 829 140 – 530 340 (Cost of sales: 15 100 + 517 530 + 12 310 – 14 600) = 298 800 (Gross profit) – 149 320 (Total overheads: 8200 + 39 350 + 4500 (18 000 × 25%) + 3940 + 1420 (14 200 × 10%) + 23 300 (22 050 + 1250) + 16 240 (81 200 × 20%) + 52 370) = 149 480 (Profit for the year)

c *Davison & Co. Statement of financial position at 31 May 2018*

Non-current assets: Machinery 39 680 (49 600 – 9920) + Office equipment 12 780 (14 200 – 1420) = 52 460

Current assets: Inventory – Finished goods 14 600 + Raw materials 9800 + Work in progress 12 200 = 36 600 + Trade receivables 64 940 + Other receivables 6400 + Cash at bank 6580 = 114 520

Total assets 166 980

Capital: Opening balance 83 200 + Profit for the year 149 480 – Drawings 81 210 = 151 470

Current liabilities: Trade payables 14 260 + Other payables 1250 = 15 510

Total capital and liabilities 166 980

SECTION 10 INCOMPLETE RECORDS

Multiple Choice Questions

1 b   **2** d   **3** c   **4** c

Shorter-Answer Questions

5 The owner may not have the skills to prepare records, or the time, or be particularly interested in having comprehensive information (two points required).

6 The minimum information required is: Opening capital (calculated from opening values of assets and liabilities), Closing capital (calculated from closing values of assets and liabilities), Drawings for the period, any Additional capital introduced during the period.

7 Purchases are: 84 490 (Payments 74 880 + Discounts received 1490 + Closing balance 6930 − Opening balance 7280 + Cash purchases 8470)

8 Profit for the year is: 19 700 [Revenue 160 000 less Cost of sales 96 000 (Average inventory 8000 × Rate of inventory turnover 12) gives Gross profit 64 000 less Expenses 44 300]

Longer-Answer Questions

9 a *Statement of affairs*

Non-current assets 74 380, Current assets 19 740 (Inventory 6770 plus Trade receivables 4730 plus Cash at bank 8240); Capital (missing figure) 80 480; Non-current liability 8500; Current liability (Trade payables) 5140

b Profit for the year is: 4030 (Closing capital 80 480 less Opening capital 82 400 add back Drawings 17 350 less Additional capital 11 400)

10 Total purchases: 70 190 [Credit purchases 68 710 (Closing trade payables 21 200 less Opening trade payables 17 340 add Payment 64 370 add Discount received 480) plus Cash purchases 1480]

Total revenue: 119 120 [Credit sales 104 250 (Closing trade receivables 15 310 less Opening trade receivables 16 490 add Receipts 105 430) add Cash sales 14 870]

11 *Workings*

Revenue: 120 630 [Credit sales 83 180 (Closing trade receivables 4480 less Opening trade receivables 3790 add Receipts 82 490) plus Cash sales 37 450]

Purchases: 39 840 [Credit purchases 36 470 (Closing trade payables 5820 less Opening trade payables 6770 add Payments 37 420) plus Cash purchases 3370]

Rent: 9 000 (Opening prepaid 200 plus Payment 9250 less Closing prepaid 450)

Wages: 23 360 (Payment 23 440 less Opening due 410 plus Closing due 330)

Income statement

Revenue 120 730 less Cost of sales 40 800 (Opening inventory 17 490 plus Purchases 39 840 less Closing inventory 16 530) to give Gross profit 79 830; less Expenses 33 360 (Rent 9 000 plus Wages 23 360); Profit for the year 45 470

12 *Workings*

Opening capital 52 960 [Non-current assets 37 450 plus Current assets 17 470 (Inventory 11 160 plus Trade receivables 2990 plus Cash at bank 3320)]; Capital (missing figure) 52 960 plus Current liabilities 1960 (Trade payables 1840 plus Electricity due 120); Statement of affairs totals 54 920

Revenue 101 570 [Credit sales 17 220 (Closing trade receivables 2320 less Opening trade receivables 2990 plus Receipts 17 890) plus Cash sales 84 350]

Purchases 44 300 (Closing trade payables 2290 less Opening trade payables 1840 plus Payments 43 850)

Electricity 3820 (Payment 3940 less Opening due 120)

Insurance 2350 (Payment 2830 less Closing prepaid 480)

Depreciation 4300 (Opening value of non-current assets 37 450 less Closing value of non-current assets 33 150)

Income statement

Revenue 101 570 less Cost of sales 40 030 (Opening inventory 11 160 plus Purchases 44 300 less Closing inventory 15 430) to give Gross profit 61 540; less Expenses 40 750 (Electricity 3820 plus Insurance 2350 plus General expenses 2810 plus Shop assistants' wages 27 470 plus Depreciation 4300); Profit for the year 20 790

Statement of affairs

Non-current assets 33 150 plus Current assets 20 400 (Inventory 15 430 plus Trade receivables 2320 plus Other receivables: Insurance 480 plus Cash at bank 2170); Capital 51 260 (Opening balance 52 960 plus Profit for the year 20 790 less Drawings 22 490) plus Current liability: Trade payables 2290; Statement of affairs totals 53 550

13 *Workings*

Opening capital 79 980 [Non-current assets 85 900 plus Current assets 22 370 (Inventory 11 160 plus Trade receivables 9730 plus Other receivables: Rent 1480); Capital (missing figure) 79 980 plus Non-current liability: Bank loan 14 000 plus Current liabilities 14 290 (Trade payables 11 990 plus Other payables: Wages 1220 plus Bank overdraft 1080); Statement of affairs totals 108 270

Revenue 190 000 (Closing trade receivables 9040 less Opening receivables 9730 plus Receipts 189 860 plus Discounts allowed 830)

Purchases 72 540 (Closing trade payables 10 200 less Opening trade payables 11 990 plus Payments 74 330)

Rent 22 950 (Payments 22 400 plus Opening prepaid 1480 less Closing prepaid 930)

Wages 51 020 (Payments 51 330 less Opening due 1220 plus Closing due 910)

Depreciation 4700 (Opening value of non-current assets 85 900 add Additions 12 000 less Closing value of non-current assets 93 200)

Closing inventory 7700 (see Income statement)

Income statement

Revenue 190 000 less Cost of sales 76 000 (i.e. 40% × revenue) (Opening inventory 11 160 plus Purchases 72 540 less Closing inventory (missing figure) 7700) gives Gross profit 114 000 (i.e. 60% × revenue) less Expenses 84 980 (Administration expenses 5480 plus Discounts allowed 830 plus Rent 22 950 plus Wages 51 020 plus Depreciation 4700); Profit for year 29 020

Statement of affairs

Non-current assets 93 200 plus Current assets 20 410 (Inventory 7700 plus Trade receivables 9040 plus Other receivables: Rent 930 plus Cash at bank 2740); Capital 90 000 (Opening balance 79 980 plus Addition 9000 plus Profit for the year 29 020 less Drawings 28 000) plus Non-current liability: Bank loan 12 500 plus Current liabilities 11 110 (Trade payables 10 200 plus Other payables: Wages 910); Statement of affairs totals 113 610

SECTION 11 ACCOUNTING RATIOS

Multiple Choice Questions

1 d   **2** b   **3** a   **4** d

Shorter-Answer Questions

5 a i   Gross profit/revenue × 100   49 000/95 000 × 100   51.58%
    ii Profit for the year/revenue × 100   19 000/95 000 × 100   20.00%
    iii Cost of sales/average inventory   46 000/15 000   3.07 times

  b The rate of inventory turnover measures how quickly the average inventory is being bought and sold in a year.

6 a i   Current assets/current liabilities   47 000/31 000   1.52:1
    ii Current assets − inventory/current liabilities   32 000/31 000   1.03:1
    iii Trade receivables/revenue × 365   30 000/192 000 × 365   57.03 days
    iv Trade payables/purchases × 365   26 000/154 000 × 365   61.62 days
    v   Profit for the year/capital employed × 100   18 000/136 000 × 100   13.24%

  b The return on capital employed measures the return on the total capital invested in the business. It is compared with a safe return, i.e. the interest received from a bank. Helen's return of 13.24% is well above bank interest and would be considered satisfactory.

Longer-Answer Questions

7 a Gross profit/revenue × 100   39 000/115 000 × 100   33.9%
  b Profit for the year/revenue × 100   19 000...
  b Profit for the year/revenue × 100   14 000/115 000 × 100   12.2%
  c Cost of sales/average inventory   76 000/17 000   4.5 times
  d Profit for the year/capital employed × 100   14 000/59 200 × 100   23.7%
  e Current assets/current liabilities   29 000/18 300   1.6:1
  f Current assets − inventory/current liabilities   23 000/18 300   1.3:1
  g Trade receivables/revenue × 365   15 500/115 000 × 365   49.2 days
  h Trade payables/purchases × 365   16 300/78 000 × 365   76.3 days

8 a i   Gross profit/revenue × 100   Larry 83/400 × 100 = 20.75%   Bob 143/520 × 100 = 27.50%
    ii Profit for year/revenue × 100   Larry 31/400 × 100 = 7.75%   Bob 73/520 × 100 = 14.04%
    iii Cost of sales/average inventory   Larry 317/32 = 9.91 times   Bob 377/43 = 8.77 times

  b Bob's business is more profitable than Larry's.
    Bob's percentage to gross profit revenue 27.5% is 6.75% higher than Larry's at 20.75%.
    This means that Bob is earning more gross profit in relation to revenue than Larry.
    Bob's percentage profit to revenue 14.04% is 6.29% higher than Larry's at 7.75%.
    This means that he is earning more profit in relation to revenue as his expenses are lower than Larry's.

9 a i The current ratio measures the business's current assets in relation to its current liabilities, and indicates whether the business has sufficient cash available to pay its short-term liabilities.

ii The liquid (acid test) ratio also measures the business's current assets in relation to its current liabilities, but excludes the inventory as this is the least liquid of the current assets. It is a more critical measurement of liquidity, and it indicates the amount of liquid assets available to pay the short-term liabilities.

b The current ratio has improved from 2:1 to 2.5:1. This indicates that the business has either increased its current assets or decreased its current liabilities.

The liquid (acid test) ratio is below 1 in both years, but it has improved slightly in 2017. This indicates that the business is holding less inventory.

The trade receivables turnover has decreased by 1 day in 2017. This indicates that the credit control has improved as trade receivables are being received quicker.

The trade payables turnover has increased by 1 day in 2017. This is due to the business taking longer to pay its suppliers.

c The current ratio in 2017 has risen above the safe level of 2:1 and it can cover its current liabilities comfortably. However, the liquid (acid test) ratio is below the safe level of 1:1 and Jessica may have difficulty in paying her suppliers.

She is also paying her trade payables before she is collecting from her trade receivables. This can lead to cash flow shortages as cash is leaving her business quicker than it is coming in.

The overall liquidity of Jessica's business could cause concern, but it would depend on the type of business she has, whether this would be considered a problem.

SECTION 12 ACCOUNTING PRINCIPLES AND POLICIES

Multiple Choice Questions

1 b   **2** a   **3** d   **4** a   **5** d   **6** a   **7** b

Shorter-Answer Questions

8 Only transactions that have a definite monetary value are recorded.

9 Every transaction has two aspects leading to the making of two entries for each transaction in the accounting system.

10 Accounting policies should be carried out in the same way year on year. For example, when calculating depreciation, a business should continue to use the same method year on year in order that the depreciation charge and the profit for the year remain comparable.

11 The printer should be recorded as an expense in the income statement according to the principle of materiality. The business is clearly quite large and the expenditure is relatively small so to write the value off over three years would be immaterial.

12 i The television should be recorded at cost price $430 as this is lower than the net realisable value of $440 (520 − 80)

  ii Prudence

13 • Comparability: enables financial statements from a wide range of countries to be compared in a valid way.

  • Relevance: Financial statements should be relevant to users making financial decisions.

  • Reliability: Information within the financial statements should be factual and free from bias, enabling a true and fair view to be presented.

  • Understandability: Financial statements should be prepared in such a way that users are able to understand the contents.

Longer-Answer Question

14 i The $2000 should be charged to drawings as this is personal expenditure. Business entity principle.

  ii The items should be valued at $340 as this is lower than the net realisable value of $365 (425 − 60). *Prudence principle*.

  iii Although the customers are very enthusiastic, no value should be placed on this in the financial statements as it is not possible to value. *Money measurement principle*.

  iv The basis of calculating depreciation should not be changed. *Consistency principle*.

  v As the goods have not been invoiced to the customer or paid for, they should not be entered in the records until this has happened. *Realisation principle*.

SECTION 14 FURTHER PRACTICE

Further Practice Questions Set 1

1 a   **2** a   **3** b   **4** a   **5** d

6 Dr – Balance b/d 750, Sales 399, Sales 144, Total 1293, Balance b/d 459
Cr – Bank 735, Discount allowed 15, Sales returns 84, Balance c/d 459, Total 1293

7 a Invoice, Sales Journal, increase 465

b Cheque, Cash book, decrease 5

c Invoice, General journal, no effect

d Cash receipt, Cash book, decrease 46

8 a *General journal*

   i   Dr – Suspense 300, Cr – Purchases 300. Purchases journal overstated

   ii   Dr – Wages 360, Cr – Suspense 360. Wages 180 credited to Wages account

   iii   Dr – Kim 256, Cr – Sales 256. Sales invoice omitted from Sales journal

   iv   Dr – C Brown 9, Cr – Purchases returns 9. Credit note 98 entered as 89

b Draft profit 36 400, add Purchases 300, less Wages 360, add Sales 256, add Purchases returns 9, Corrected profit 36 605

9 a *General Journal*

   Dr – Bank 1042, Bad debts 4168
   Cr – Julia Jones 5210
   Cheque received for 20c in $, and balance written off as bad debt

b The provision for doubtful debts is profit set aside to cover uncertain future bad debts. In the statement of financial position it is deducted from the trade receivables. This reduces their value and shows them at a more realistic figure.

10 a Gross profit = Profit for the year 5500 add Expenses 18 000 = 23 500.
Revenue 55 000, less Gross profit 23 500 = Cost of sales 31 500

b Gross profit 23 500/Revenue 55 000 × 100 = 42.7%

c Current assets: Inventory 16 000, Trade receivables 12 400 = 28 400
Current liabilities: Trade payables 7000, Bank overdraft 5600 = 12 600
Working capital ratio: Current assets 28 400/Current liabilities 12 600 = 2.3:1

d Current assets less Inventory 12 400/Current liabilities 12 600 = 1:1

11 a i   Cost of sales 90 000/100 × 125 = revenue 112 500
   ii   Revenue 112 500, less Cost of sales 90 000 = Gross profit 22 500
   iii Gross profit 22 500, less Expenses 12 900 = Profit for the year 9600

b i Gross profit 22 500/Revenue 112 500 × 100 = 20%

ii Profit for the year 9600/Revenue 112 500 × 100 = 8.5%

iii Cost of sales 90 000/average Inventory 19 735 = 4.6 times

iv Profit for the year 9600/Capital employed 120 000 = 8%

c i Both the percentage gross margin (26.4% to 20%) and the profit margin (12.3% to 8.5%) have deteriorated. This means that Ahmed is making less profit on his trading operations.

ii Ahmed's return on capital employed has also got worse, decreasing from 10.4% to 8%. This means that he is earning less return on his investment in the business.

d i Ahmed could increase his profit for the year by reducing his overheads.

ii Ahmed could reduce his capital employed by increasing his drawings, or by repaying or reducing the non-current liabilities.

12 a i *Subscriptions account* Dr – Balance b/d 180, Income and expenditure 12 240, Balance c/d 260, Total 12 680, Balance b/d 220

Cr – Balance b/d 320, Cash 12 140, Balance c/d 220, Total 12 680, Balance b/d 260

ii *Refreshments account* Income – Revenue 6436

Less Cost of sales – Opening inventory 530, add Purchases (3250 +720 - 660) 3310, less Closing inventory 580 = 3260

Gross profit: Revenue 6436 less Cost of sales 3260 = 3176

Profit on refreshments: Gross profit 3176, less Wages 800 = 2376

b Equipment: Opening balance 6000, add Purchases 7820 = 13 820, less Closing balance 12 200 Depreciation = 1620

c Revaluation

13 a *General Journal*

i Dr – Suspense 74, Cr – Purchases returns 74. Purchases returns journal undercast.

ii Dr – Suspense 90, Cr – Wages 90. Wages 670 recorded as 760.

iii Dr – J Brown 350, Cr – W Brown 350. Sales entered in error in W Brown's account

iv Dr – Suspense 175, Cr – Rent 175. Rent 175 recorded twice.

v Dr – Suspense 17, Cr – Discount received 17. Discount received undercast.

b *Suspense account* Dr – Purchases returns 74, Wages 90, rent 175, Discount received 17, total 356

Cr – Difference in Trial balance 356, total 356

14 Assets: Non-current assets 24 000, Trade receivables 12 230, Inventory 5140, Insurance prepaid 380, total 41 750

Liabilities: Trade payables 8670, General expenses accrued 140, Bank overdraft 1170, Bank loan 2500 Total 12 480

Capital: Assets 41 750, less Liabilities 12 480 = 29 270

Assets and liabilities at this date

Further Practice Questions Set 2

1 b.   **2** c   **3** c   **4** d   **5** d

6 a *Alan. Income statement for the year ended 30 June 2018*

Revenue 323 400 – Returns inwards 2510 = 320 890 – Cost of sales 173 090 [62 000 + (166 800 – 1290 – 1900) – 1020 – 51 500] = Gross profit 147 800 – Operating expenses 83 149 ((28 840 + 1680) + (31 100 – 2400) + 12 420 +(58 900 x 10%) + (38 000 – 13 600) × 20% (24 000 × 8% × 4/12) + ((38 400 × 1%) – 285) = Profit for the year 64 651.

b *Alan. Statement of financial position at 30 June 2018*

Non-current assets: 50 430 (Motor vehicles 38 000 – 13 600 – 4880) + (Equipment 58 900 – 22 100 – 5890)

Current assets: Inventory 51 500 + Trade receivables (38 400 – 384) + Other receivables 2400

Total assets: 142 346 (50 430 + 91 916)

Capital and liabilities

Capital account 93 056 (b/f 73 245 + Profit 64 651 – Drawings (42 940 + 1900)

Current liabilities: 25 690 (Trade payables 18 180 + Other payables (1680 + 640) + Bank overdraft 4790)

Non-current liabilities: Bank loan 24 000

Total capital and liabilities 152 346 (93 056 + 25 290 + 24 000)

c Prudence

d Wear and tear, obsolescence, damage, passage of time, depletion.

7 a *Arthur and Ben. Appropriation account for the year ended 31 August 2018*

Profit for the year 44 212

Add: Interest on drawings 2988 (A 1650, B 1338)

Deduct: Interest on capital 5000 (A, 3000, B, 2000)

Partner's salary 8000

Profit available 34 200

Split: A (3/5) 20 520; B (2/5) 13 680

b *Partners' capital accounts*

Partner A

Debit   Closing balance c/d 60 000

Credit Opening balance b/d 60 000

(Note Closing balance b/d is Credit 60 000)

Partner B

Debit Closing balance c/d 40 000

Credit Opening balance b/d 30 000; Bank 10 000

(Note Closing balance b/d is Credit 40 000

c *Partners' current accounts*

Partner A

Debit Drawing 27 500; Interest on drawings 1650; Closing balance c/d 20 700

Credit Opening balance 26 330; Interest on capital 3000; Share of profit 20 520

(Note Closing balance b/d is Credit 20 700

Partner B

Debit Opening balance 6180; Drawings 22 300; Interest on drawings 1338

Credit Salary 8000; Interest on capital 2000; Share of profit 13 680; Closing balance c/d 6138

(Note Closing balance b/d is Debit 6138)

d The debit balance brought forward on Ben's current account means that he has withdrawn more than he has accrued in profits, salary and interest on capital. The same situation exists at the end of the year. He has taken more drawings than his share of profits.

8 a *Sagbo & Co. Manufacturing account for the year ended 30 April 2018*

Opening inventory raw materials 28 420 + Purchases 214 110 + Carriage inwards 1840 – Closing inventory 25 600 = 218 770 (Raw materials consumed) + Direct wages 43 750 = 262 520 (Prime cost) + 92 100 (Total factory overheads: (28 200 + 1430) + 11 100 (14 800 × 75%) + 10 080 (12 600 × 80%) +5090 + 33 600 [(45 620 – 3620) × 4/5]) + 2600 = 354 620 + 12 360 (Opening WIP) – 9370 (Closing WIP) = 357 610 (Cost of production).

b Direct costs are those that can be associated with an individual product, for example, raw materials or direct labour to make the product. Indirect costs are those costs that are associated with the manufacture, but cannot be directly associated with an individual product, for example, light, heat and power, machinery maintenance, etc.

c The accruals principle has been applied in providing for the accrual on the factory supervisor's salary and the prepayment on rent and rates. This ensures that only those costs applicable to the current financial year are included in the manufacturing account.

9 a *Subscriptions account*

Debit Opening balance b/d 960; income and expenditure (difference) 5760; closing balance c/d 560

Credit Bank 6800; Closing balance c/d 480

(Note Closing balances b/d are Debit 480, Credit 560)

b The accumulated fund of a club or society is represented by the difference between the assets and liabilities. It is the total of the annual surpluses made by the organisation over the years. It is the equivalent of the capital of a trading business.

10 a Gross profit = 183 [340 – (52 + 165 – 60)]

b Profit for the year = 47 (183 – 136)

c	**i**	(Gross profit / revenue) × 100	53.8%
	ii	(Profit for the year / revenue) × 100	13.8%
	iii	Current assets / current liabilities	1.8:1
	iv	Current assets excluding inventory / current liabilities	0.9:1
	v	(Trade receivables / credit sales) × 365	59.0 days
	vi	(Trade payables / credit purchases) × 365	70.8 days
	vii	(Profit for the year / capital employed) × 100	26.1%

d Increase selling prices or reduce purchase prices